# Wisdom

## What you should HAVE learned as a teenager but didn't

Scriptures studied, life's observations and experiences, academic training at several universities, consultation with other brilliant minds, and more than forty years of ministry and life coaching have produced these lessons. Though I have searched and researched for this production, I do not declare originality for any of the content of these materials.

This book, nor parts thereof, may not be reproduced in any form, stored in a retrieval system, or transmitted in any form by any means—electronic, mechanical, photocopy, recording, or otherwise—without prior written permission of the publisher except as provided by United States copyright law.

Unless otherwise quoted, all Scripture quotations are from the New American Standard Version of the Bible. Copyright © 1960, 1962, 1963, 1968, 1971, 1972, 1973, 1975, 1977, 1995 2020 by the Lockman Foundation, a Corporation Not for Profit

Copyright © 2024 by www.JohnDavisMarshall.com All rights reserved.

# Table of Contents

The Second Most Important Exercise of Wisdom .............................. 1

**Section One**  **Gather Internal Wisdom** ..................................... 11

        Studying ........................................................... 13
        Speed Reading ............................................... 15
        Note and Test Taking .................................... 19
        Learning .......................................................... 21

**Section Two**  **Honor Eternal Wisdom** ....................................... 27

        Choose to Believe the Bible ........................ 29
        Creation vs. Evolution ................................. 35
        God .................................................................. 41
        Morality vs. No Morality ............................ 45

**Section Three**  **Share Intellectual Wisdom** ............................. 51

        Gathering Information ............................... 53
        Writing ........................................................... 55
        Publishing ...................................................... 63
        Parenting ....................................................... 81
        Peer pressure ............................................... 85

The First Most Important Exercise of Wisdom ................................ 89

# The Second Most Important Exercise of Wisdom

## The Second Most Important Exercise of Wisdom

Deciding whom you will marry is the second most important decision that you will ever make. Your married companion will encourage, assist, and enable you to propel forward and upward or backward and downward. Since dating is the most often used process to decide whom to marry, we address dating as an exercise of wisdom.

A direction and definition for dating are always in order. Dating is the social sifting process through which a man gets to know the character and characteristics of a woman, intending for her to become his wife. Also, dating is the social sifting process through which a woman gets to know the character and characteristics of a man, intending for him to become her husband. Therefore, as I will be addressing it, dating is designed for those who intend to marry. Dating just for social companionship, without intending to become married, is outside of my scope of reference. However, this writing does not denounce the validity of the latter.

Divine Dating! Dating should be a sifting process not a sorting process. When you sort, you rank and keep all. When you sift, you eliminate all except the final one.

Suppose you date for a while and rank that person to be a perspective spouse. Considering all that you have discovered, you believe that this person is a viable candidate for you, so you rank that individual as a perspective spouse. In the meantime, the dating relationship sours yet you retain that person's ranking as a potential spouse for you.

Sometime later, you marry another individual. When the newlywed gloss wears off and you reevaluate your spouse, you are liable to rank your spouse lower than your previous perspective spouse. Now, how do you feel?

Most everyone dates at an artificial level. They highly overrate and over-rank the person they are dating. Therefore, when they become married, their positives fall down, and their negatives stand up.

The ranking of a perceived-to-be-good spouse within your subconscious mind may provide confusing data that will regularly irritate your marriage. Far too often, even if only for a moment, you will wonder how life would have been if you had married that other person from your past. Unfortunately to their detriment, far too many men and women use dating as a sorting process rather than a sifting process.

Many of the people you meet should never be brought into your life. Some are good people but are not good for you. Some are not good for you currently. Others with their present disposition are not good for anyone at any time. Why waste your time? The mature person does not ask, "Is it right or wrong to date this person?" but rather, "Is it best for me to date this person now?"

Before you start sifting, make two lists. List #1 should contain the maximum of all the character and characteristics that you would like to have in your wife or husband. List #2 contains the minimum of character and characteristics that you must have in your wife or husband. For example, if as a man, you positively desire never to marry a woman who has three "baby daddies," why start dating her who has three children? If, as a woman you definitively desire never to marry a man who has three "baby mommas," why start dating him who has three children?

Before you critique your potential spouse, make sure that you qualify on your own critique list. If you are not a person of character, you will have difficulty identifying a person of character. Being a person of character will enable you to show grace and mercy toward those who are imperfect.

Before you begin making your lists, study God's approved character and characteristic list. Train yourself to see and value what God sees and values. What does God look for in a man or woman who will become married?

As you date and discover reasons why this person should not become your spouse, remove that person from the prospective list. Sift that person out of potentiality. Do not sort and keep that person as a "if no one else shows up,"" I will come back to that person." Use the sifting process, not the sorting process, to eliminate individuals from the potential spouse list.

**For the female**

When He needed men to allocate daily resources to women, God chose men who had good reputations and were full of the spirit and wisdom (see Acts 6:3). Why would you choose any less? When God needed men to become example leaders within the church, once again, He specified the character and characteristics (see 1 Timothy 3:1-7, Titus 1:5-9).

**For example, God wanted church leaders to:**

He must share his wisdom visually.
He must be patient and not be a brawler.
He must be vigilant.
He must be not given to wine.
He must be no striker.
He must be not greedy of filthy lucre.
He must be not covetous.
He must be hospitable.
He has a good reputation from outside the church.

He must share his wisdom verbally.
He must know what the scriptures teach.
He must be willing teach that which he knows.

Look for a spouse that radiates this type character these characteristics.

[MAKE SURE THAT YOU OBTAIN A COPY OF MY BOOK: A QUEEN In SEARCH OF A KING, "Go head and ask Him for a date"!

**For the male**
King Lemuel's mother gave him the best criteria for selecting a wife. Just learn Proverbs 31. I have included some highlights below.

*$^{10}$An excellent wife, who can find her? . . . $^{11}$ The heart of her husband trusts in her, . . . $^{12}$ She does him good and not evil All the days of her life. . . . And works with her hands in delight. . . . $^{15}$ And she rises while it is still night And gives food to her household, . . . . She extends her hand to the poor, And she stretches out her hands to the needy. $^{21}$ She is not afraid of the snow for her*

household,. . . ²⁵ Strength and dignity are her clothing, And she smiles at the future. ²⁶ She opens her mouth in wisdom, And the teaching of kindness is on her tongue. ²⁷ She watches over the activities of her household, And does not eat the bread of idleness. . . . ³⁰ Charm is deceitful and beauty is vain, But a woman who fears the Lord, she shall be praised.

## Should believers date those who are not believers?

God intended for practically all men and women to become married. That dictates that some form of socializing, i.e. dating, would be necessary to lead them to become married. God intended for dating and marriage to be within the normal grasp of every person. He never intended for them to constantly need the professional help of a psychologist to date and remain successfully married. Although the occasional need for a therapist may arise, this would be the exception, not the rule. Everyone, however, must think correctly and think thoroughly about substantive issues relative to nature and the manner of their relationship.

You have noticed that friendship and communication are significant elements for a quality marriage. How will two people become friends except if they communicate and get to know the heart of each other? Therefore, dating in such a way as to learn the heart of your prospective spouse just makes sense.

After becoming the right date, you must then date the right way. What does the word of God say about dating? The word of God emphasizes a pertinent principle that should govern your dating. Read the text of this scripture carefully so that you can grasp it. **"Do not sharply rebuke an older man, but rather appeal to him as a father, to the younger men as brothers, the older women as mothers, and the younger women as sisters, in all purity"** (1 Timothy 5:1-2).

God wants young men to treat older women in all purity, just as they would their biological mothers. He wants younger men to treat younger women in all purity, just as they would treat their biological sisters. If you are an older woman, you must not only expect to be but also appreciate being treated as a mother in all purity. If you are a younger woman, you too must not only expect to be but also appreciate being treated as a sister *in all purity*. Therefore, as you date, think and do what you would think and do with your brother. Would you dress provocatively to go to the movie with your brother? Would you sit on your brother's lap and sensually caress his chest? Would you gaze for hours into your brother's eyes while feeling the warmth of his breath?

The bible never discusses who one should date but certainly provides guidelines for how one should date. You can limit your dating experiences just to those who are believers. And God will approve. However, you can expand your dating experiences to include those who are not believers. And again, God will approve.

During the dating process you should sift, looking for a spiritually compassionate progressive thinker. When you discover such a person, you may need to introduce him/her to better alternate options than he/she has heretofore chosen. Therefore, the believer can invite the nonbeliever to explore the world of belief in Jesus Christ. When the nonbeliever embraces faith in Jesus, you now have an additional layer of connectedness. However, if the nonbeliever rejects faith in Jesus, you know that you will not be compatible. Therefore, you need to cease dating that individual.

Now, some will say, but aren't you setting yourself up for failure? The problem surfaces when believers' feelings override their faith. But dating is only for those who have matured to the point where their faith rules their feelings. Otherwise, you are just asking for disaster. When faith rules, you can cut ties and walk away whenever you have reason to believe that your spiritual best interest is not being served.

Now, some will say, but I [and no one else] am not that mature. Then I do not recommend that you date anyone. Invest your energies in growing spiritually while God is preparing a spouse for you. As I state in my book A Queen In Search of a King, Go ahead and ask Him for a date, prepare to become a woman, and then God will present you as a wife. The same is also true for men.

**Build a Permanent Character Based Dating Relationship**
God brought Paul and Timothy together in ministry (Acts 16:1-3). From their first encounter, they formed a lifelong bond. Christian relationships should last. We ought to develop lifelong bonds of fellowship and friendship. How? First, build your relationship upon character. Character – the willingness to do right as God defines right regardless of the cost.

Paul and Timothy built their relationship upon character. Paul said it this way, *"For I have no one else of kindred spirit who will <u>genuinely be concerned</u>*

*for your welfare. For they all seek after their own interests, not those of Christ Jesus. But you know of his proven worth, that he served with me in the furtherance of the gospel like a child serving his father"* (Philippians 2:20-22; Acts 16:1, 1 Corinthians 4:17).

Second, build your relationship upon characteristics. Characteristics – redemptive compatible qualities.

Paul and Timothy built their relationship upon characteristics. Paul said it this way, *"For I have no one else of kindred spirit who will genuinely be concerned for your welfare. For they all seek after their own interests, not those of Christ Jesus. But you know of his proven worth, that he served with me in the furtherance of the gospel like a child serving his father"* (Philippians 2:20-22).

Third, build your relationship upon chemistry. Chemistry – invisible and intangible personality connectedness.

Paul and Timothy built their relationship upon chemistry. Paul said it this way, *"For I have no one else of kindred spirit who will genuinely be concerned for your welfare. For they all seek after their own interests, not those of Christ Jesus. But you know of his proven worth, that he served with me in the furtherance of the gospel like a child serving his father"* (Philippians 2:20-22)

Fourth, build your relationship upon chivalry. Chivalry – courtesy, thoughtfulness, compassion.

Paul and Timothy built their relationship upon chivalry. Paul said it this way, *"For I have no one else of kindred spirit who will genuinely be concerned for your welfare. For they all seek after their own interests, not those of Christ Jesus"* (Philippians 2:20-21).

Relationships just seem to deteriorate over time. Compare your relationship now to your high-school friends. Why?

We are building our relationships upon culture conditioning rather than character conditioning. Culture continually corrupts relationships.

Culture gives us the reverse order. Culture says chivalry, chemistry, and characteristics and rarely proceeds to character. Now you know why dating does not lead to marriage.

# SECTION

## GATHER INTERNAL WISDOM

# STUDYING

**Studying**

A wise educator once said, "Studying is the process that students use to decide what to learn, what to remember, and what to recall." Therein, your long-term memory and long-term memory retrieval become crucial. Studying profits little if you fail to retain in memory what you retrieved from the notes.

Studying does not have to be a complicated process. Ask yourself a simple question: Are you a visual (see), auditory (hear), or kinesthetic (hands-on) learner? What if you aren't sure? Well, think back to all those classes you have taken throughout your academic career. There were forms of learning that came much easier to you than other forms. Which forms were easier for you? Think about your favorite teachers and/or favorite subjects. Which style of teaching took place herein? Therein is your learning style. Develop study skills tailored to your unique learning style to achieve more productive results.

Expand your vocabulary. Learn at least one new word each week. Master the verbs. Verbs are the power words. Think and talk in terms of the power of action.

For students who are in school, there is no such thing as a "no-homework" day. You must always study every day (night) at home. When I attended secondary school, my parents demanded that I bring every textbook home every evening, even when there was no homework due. My mother would ask, "Do you have homework?" I would answer no. She would ask what pages you studied today. I would say pages 14-22. She would say go read pages 23-30.

During my college enrollment, I worked a full-time job. Therefore, I had to be very efficient. I discovered that if I would, reread study notes and materials as soon after class as possible, the more I would retain. The sooner you can read and study, the more you are likely to retain. More significant learning occurs while the material is fresh and clear in the mind. Study for short periods. You will likely retain very little when you prolong studying until you are exhausted.

# SPEED READING

**Speed-Read for Comprehension**

It has been said that speed reading improves not only your overall reading process but also your reading comprehension. That's because practicing speed reading accelerates brain processes and boosts memory, leading to increased comprehension. Learn to read. Learn to read well. Learn to speed-read for comprehension.

Improve your reading comprehension. There exists a cause-and-effect relationship between reading rate (speed) and comprehension rate. Speed reading is about controlling your reading rate, not just about passing by more words. Faster reading makes the reading more interesting, which increases comprehension.

Read the first sentence in each paragraph more slowly. Then speed up reading the other sentences. Usually, the first sentence is a topic sentence containing the paragraph's main idea.

- Eliminate vocalization and sub-vocalization while reading.

- Skim over the writing, read the writing, and skim over the writing again.

- Read by focusing on phrases rather than individual words. Practice by reading newspaper columns.

- Use an index card. Place the card under the line in which you are reading.

- Constantly, move the card down through the writing, setting the pace for your eyes.

- Practice, practice, and practice.

## Underlining

Strategic underling reduces study time by at least 50%. Underline only pertinent information. Do not underline general information that you will automatically conclude. Select the words that make up full sentences [see the examples below]. When you review or study, only read the underlined. Now you see how proper underling will reduce your reading time by at least 50%.

## The Trail of Tears

The <u>original inhabitants of</u> what is now <u>Kentucky and Tennessee,</u> were an industrious people who <u>lived</u> mainly <u>by hunting and farming</u>. They were <u>called Cherokees by the Europeans who</u> first <u>made contact</u> with them, <u>after settling</u> along <u>the East Cost in the early 1600's</u>. These first meetings between European traders and Cherokees were friendly, but would eventually have devastating consequences for the Native Americans. The <u>Europeans brought goods</u> for trading, but they also brought <u>smallpox</u>, a disease that had been <u>unknown in North America before their arrival</u>. <u>This disease</u> left the body <u>covered with sores</u> and was <u>often fatal</u>. <u>In 1745</u>, a smallpox <u>epidemic</u> struck the Cherokee people and <u>killed</u> more than <u>half the population</u>. And that was just the beginning of the Cherokee people's woes!

<u>The</u> United States <u>government recognized the Cherokee Nation as a</u> separate <u>country and acknowledged its right to sign treaties</u>, or legally binding agreements, <u>with other countries</u>. In treaty after treaty, <u>the Cherokees gave more</u> and more of their <u>land to the</u> United States <u>government</u> in return <u>for the right to evict anyone who settled illegally on the remaining land</u>. Despite that, <u>settlers ignored</u> these agreements <u>and continued to move onto Cherokee land</u>. The United States <u>government did not</u> even <u>pretend to be impartial in the disputes</u> that arose as a result. <u>The appeals</u> of the Cherokee leaders <u>fell on deaf ears, and the theft of their land continued</u> unabated. <u>By 1828, the</u> Cherokee <u>Nation was one-tenth the size it had been a hundred years earlier</u>.

<u>In 1835, an agent</u> of the United States government <u>persuaded twenty Cherokees to sign</u> one <u>final treaty</u>. According to its terms, the <u>Cherokees would get five million dollars for leaving</u> the last of their land <u>and moving</u> almost <u>a thousand miles west</u>. The Cherokees <u>signers had no authority</u> to act for the entire Cherokee Nation, <u>but this fact was</u> brushed aside as

irrelevant by those in the government who wanted the land. The chief justice of the United States declared the agreement a sham. His opinion infuriated President Andrew Jackson, who replied, "The chief justice has made his decision; now let him enforce it."

Precisely two years after the signing of the agreement, on the orders of the president, two thousand heavily armed United States soldiers arrived and drove the Cherokee families from their homes. Nearly twenty thousand people were forced to trek more than nine hundred miles west into what is now Oklahoma. They went mostly on foot, and it has been estimated that about four thousand Native Americans died on the journey, which became known as the "trail of tears." In a sense, though the Cherokees had traveled an even longer and even more sorrowful trail, this journey in time began when the unsuspecting Cherokees first greeted the Europeans as friends.

**Harvest of Shame**

Many Americans are lucky to have ample supplies of fruits and vegetables in their supermarkets twelve months a year. Did you ever wonder who picks this food? An estimated three-quarters of a million men, women and children travel the United States picking asparagus and strawberries in Washington State, citrus fruits in Florida, apples in New York state, and many kinds of vegetables in California. These laborers are called migrant farm workers because they move from place to place, wherever crops need picking. Most would prefer permanent full-time employment, but it is not often availed to them.

The workday is strenuous; pickers bend and stoop, often under a blazing hot sun, from seven in the morning until seven at night. Their only respite may be a twenty-minute lunch break. Because it is considered menial work for low wages, laborers are paid only when they pick. If it rains, or if they are too sick to work, they get nothing. What's more they cannot get adequate medical treatment when they are ill or injured.

The children suffer because their education is disrupted as they move from school to school. In fact, only one student in ten graduates from high school. The young people often drop out of school altogether to toil in the fields alongside their parents. Here, they may risk exposure to chemical pesticides sprayed on crops. One California study showed cancer among migrant workers' children at twelve times the normal rate.

In the 1960s, laborers in California began to agitate for better working conditions, but the growers were indifferent to their demands. So the migrant workers, under the leadership of two Mexican-Americans, Cesar Chavez and Dolores Fernandez Huerta, formed a labor union called the United Farm Workers of America. When growers tried to ignore the union, it rallied for strikes and organized boycotts of California lettuce and grapes. It took years of struggle, many organized marches, and sometimes violent clashes. However, in the end, most of the growers capitulated and in 1966 recognized the union's right to represent workers. Despite the union's efforts, conditions have improved only slightly since the 1960s. One notable accomplishment has been the creation of the East Coast Migrant Head Start Project, which administers many child-care centers for migrants. Established in 1974, by 2002 it operated eighty-six centers in twelve states. Though this helped to improve conditions in some areas, the need for more programs is urgent. Educational programs could lower illiteracy rates among migrant workers and their families. Outreach programs could also help to improve migrant workers' living conditions. Many workers live without running water and electricity. These necessary additions and minimal repairs to their homes would help to turn their dwellings from inadequate hovels into acceptable community housing.

On the day after Thanksgiving 1960, CBS aired a film about migrant farm workers that shocked the Nation. Sadly, if the film were to be shown today, very little of it would seem out of date. And its title would be as apt today as it was then. The film was called *Harvest of Shame.*

## Seating in Class
Always sit on the front row. The closer you sit to the instructor or the source of information, the fewer distractions you must contend with. A reduction in distractions may increase the percentage of information you retain in memory. Also, instructors may perceive that students who sit nearer to the front are more interested and are, therefore, more willing to assist them.

## Relating To Your Instructor
Ask your instructor questions until the information becomes clear in your mind. You are paying your instructors to teach you by taxes or tuition. You have a right to insist that they perform their job so that you can understand the material they present.

After the class period ends, discuss with the instructor the information just presented. Especially, talk about the relevancy of the information just received. Once again, the instructor may perceive that your interest warrants a greater favor or benefit of the doubt when grading your schoolwork.

# NOTE AND TEST TAKING

**Note and Test Taking**

During class, you may write phrases, but immediately after class, rewrite them into complete sentences. Writing and rewriting improve retention and comprehension.

The night before an examination, get a good night's rest. Retire early enough to get adequate sleep. Remove all anxieties before falling asleep. Tell yourself that you are going to do well on the exam the next day because you know that you know what you know. On the exam day, arise promptly and eat a nutritious breakfast. If possible, avoid taking an exam on an empty stomach.

Read and study quietly until exam time. Avoid the anxiety society. Do not engage in worry conversations with other students about their perceptions and misperceptions of the exam. Avoid worrying and fear-laden people who release their negative energy into the atmosphere. If possible, do not enter the test-taking area until after all has quieted and the test-taking has started.

Practice relaxed breathing during the exam. This keeps the circulation flourishing and reduces mental tension and stress. Close your eyes, breathe deeply, rotate your shoulders, and stretch your neck for improved blood flow and relaxation.

Always tell yourself that you will do well on the test and in life. Restate and rethink negatives into positives. Power talks will make your mind stronger and tougher and your self-confidence indestructible. On the night before a challenging experience, visualize an increase in confidence. Walk through the routine of expressing your confidence. On the morning of, recreate the position of increased confidence. You can believe in yourself. Despite the seeming impossibilities, you can condition yourself to believe in yourself totally. Therefore, when the alarm goes off, never hit the snooze button. This is a terrible habit that starts off the day resisting.

# > LEARNING

**LEARNING**

The famous literary critic, T.S. Eliot, asked, "Where is the wisdom we have lost in knowledge? Where is the knowledge we have lost in information?"

Though wisdom is greater than the learning of knowledge and information, wisdom starts with learning. Wisdom is the capacity, ability, and willingness to regulate the factors and forces to produce a favorable outcome. Wisdom is the ability and willingness to relate and apply instructions properly. Wisdom rests upon an accurate understanding of the information. Accept the information and use the instructions so that you introduce wisdom into every aspect of your life. Wisdom is the fruit that swings from the leaves of learning.

Learning is acquiring knowledge of a skill through study, instructions, and experience. Most often, learning results in a lasting behavior change. Learning requires thinking. Thinking engages the mind. Engaging the mind through mental gymnastics leads to greater learning. Greater learning may result in increased wisdom. Both take place in the mind.

The mind consists of a **conscious component.** Our conscious mind receives, reviews, and retains *a small portion of the data* that appears to us. It consists of our recallable memory. Consciousness is a term that refers to the relationship between the mind and the world with which it interacts. It has been defined as subjectivity, awareness, the ability to experience or to feel, wakefulness, having a sense of selfhood, and the executive control system of the mind.

Also, the mind consists of a **subconscious component**. Our subconscious mind receives, reviews, and retains *all the data* that appears to us. Our subconscious mind consists of our recallable and suppressed memory. Through hypnosis, data that has been suppressed in the subconscious mind is brought back into the conscious mind.

The subconscious mind is the most potent part of your mind because it controls your destiny. While the conscious mind oversees thoughts and actions under your control, the subconscious mind takes charge of your feelings and emotions. How you direct your subconscious mind will greatly determine and affect the quality of your life.

Your subconscious mind stores knowledge through repetition. When you constantly tell yourself about an idea or a belief, your subconscious mind will ultimately accept it. Positive affirmations can, therefore, effectively achieve what you want in life because your thoughts control your actions. If you speak unkindly about yourself, you tend to feel inferior and insecure. So, try to appreciate your good qualities and compliment yourself on your positive traits. Do this positive self-talk as often as you can; your subconscious mind will also positively see you. The self-confidence that results from a positive outlook of yourself can lead to success, prosperity, and happiness in life.

The subconscious mind is also known for its power to heal. Doctors say that the mind and the body always work together to regain a person's health. A patient has a greater chance of recovering from an illness if he believes that he will rather than if he believes that he will not.

In addition, the mind has a **conscience component**. Our conscience mind receives, reviews, and retains *data that is assigned moral and/or ethical value*. It also consists of our belief system, the product of accepted teachings.

Conscience is a sense of right and wrong guiding a person's actions, *Oxford Mini Dictionary & Thesaurus; (2008)*. This dictionary also gave words such as morals, principles, ethics, standards, scruples, qualms, and compunction. The conscience is an inner level that is uniquely furnished inside oneself that includes a feeling, an emotion, a thought, and an inner motive like intuition. To go more in-depth, it is like an "obedient measure" and "moral law" that provides the right or wrong mode from good or bad.

**Feed Your Mind**

Read: Read more and more. Place a book at every sitting location. Read quality materials. In addition to reading light materials for relaxation, read materials by which you can learn new ideas. Read material that challenges you to think differently, divergently, and even dissentingly. Reading is an experience wherein information is brought into the mind.

- ❖ Always be open to learning.
- ❖ Read self-help books.
- ❖ Surround yourself with encouraging friends and colleagues that help push you in a more positive direction.
- ❖ By refocusing on positive thoughts, block negative thoughts when they creep into your head.
- ❖ Listen to podcasts, YouTube, and/or media that offer insight on personal growth, spirituality, or positive affirmations.
- ❖ Change your internal vibration by changing the signals you send out to others.
- ❖ Forgive and be kind to yourself for past mistakes. Apply this principle to others. While you can't change the past, you can change how you feel about yourself and your thoughts going forward.

**Stretch Your Mind**

Your mind is a reservoir of creative potential, just waiting for you to nurture and develop it. Too many people say they aren't innovative. I say - they either haven't developed their creativity or are looking at creativity through a narrowly focused lens.

Imagine your mind as a rubber band. As you put creative ideas, dreams, and inspiration into it, your mind stretches and flexes around the new thoughts. As the mind is stretched, it becomes more capable of stretching and flexing, able to accommodate and generate more and greater ideas and creativity. I have a sister who is three years older than I. She taught me her school classwork. Therefore, I went through school three years ahead in learning and knowledge. Neither elementary nor high school classwork challenged me, but my sister's teaching me her classwork had already stretched my mind.

When my sister entered high school, our dad purchased a manual typewriter for her. She insisted that I learn the keyboard rather than peck around on it. When I took the typing course in high school, I was very proficient because my sister had stretched my mind years earlier. Technical school in the Air Force was reduced by six weeks because I was already a great typist. As an author and publisher, the ability to type proficiently has saved me thousands of dollars. Stretching your mind early in life may help you stretch your money later.

My brother did for my sister what she did for me. People thought that we were more intelligent than most. We were not smarter; we were just wise enough to maximize our minds.

I have always enjoyed learning. As a 6th-grade boy, I learned Gregg shorthand. It proved to be an exciting way to stretch my mind.

**Memorization**

Memorize poetry. Learn songs, especially gospel songs. Sing during worship without reading the words. Force yourself to recall what you read. Challenge yourself to remember larger and larger blocks of data. Refuse to write unimportant data that you can quickly retrieve with memory. Remember more and more information. Rote memory is not real learning; rote learning expands one's memory capacity.

Force yourself to remember phone numbers. Dial them without looking at the number. Memorize credit and debit card numbers. Memorize bank account numbers. Remember mathematic and algebraic formulas. Perform math and algebra without using a calculator.

# SECTION

## HONOR ETERNAL WISDOM

# CHOOSE TO BELIEVE THE BIBLE

**Choose to Believe the Bible**

> *[16] For we did not follow cleverly devised tales when we made known to you the power and coming of our Lord Jesus Christ, but we were eyewitnesses of His majesty. [17] For when He received honor and glory from God the Father, such a declaration as this was made to Him by the Majestic Glory: "This is My beloved Son with whom I am well pleased"— [18] and we ourselves heard this declaration made from heaven when we were with Him on the holy mountain. [19] And so we have the prophetic word made more sure, to which you do well to pay attention as to a lamp shining in a dark place, until the day dawns and the morning star arises in your hearts. [20] But know this first of all, that no prophecy of Scripture becomes a matter of someone's own interpretation, [21] for no prophecy was ever made by an act of human will, but men moved by the Holy Spirit spoke from God.* 2 Peter 2:16-21

Some say they cannot trust anything man wrote in a book because man is fallible and subject to error. For those, consistency demands that they cannot believe anything written in any book because a fallible man wrote everything written in any book. If you can't believe a fallible man, you cannot believe yourself because you know you are also fallible. You are fallible, yet you believe you. How can fallible you believe yourself while not believing another fallible person?

Some say they only believe in science. Science must be observable, measurable, and repeatable. Science is not the way you prove history or historical documents. You prove historical documents by the evidentiary method, not scientifically.

You evaluate the reliability, corroboration, and internal and external evidence. Consider a witness's reliability and trustworthiness. Is the written document falsifiable? What contradictions and what confirmations and affirmations are in the writing?

God is the sovereign Authority and has placed the Bible as the highest tribunal authority on earth. Therefore, I choose to believe the Bible.

I believe the Bible because it is a reliable collection of historical documents.

The Bible is reliable. Though he was not an eyewitness, Luke researched from eyewitnesses and provided an accurate, valid chronology of the events (Luke 1:1-4). Mark reported the facts; Matthew persuaded the Jews that Jesus was the Messiah, while John was evangelistic.

The Bible is a reliable collection. African culture penetrates the Bible, destroying the hellish myth that it is a European-written (white man's) book. It is a reliable collection of writings gathered from three different continents: Africa ~ the Eunuch was from **Ethiopia** on the continent of **Africa** (Acts 8:27), Asia ~ the disciples engaged in the dispute were from **Jerusalem** on the continent of **Asia** (Acts 15:1-4) and Europe ~ the apostle Paul left **Athens** and went to **Corinth** – both are on the continent of **Europe** (Acts 18:1).

The Bible, some 1,500 years in the making, was initially written in three (3) languages - Hebrew, Greek, and Aramaic by forty (40) authors from various backgrounds. It contains sixty-six (66) volumes about hundreds of subjects, topics, and ideas.

The Bible is a reliable collection of historical documents. The Bible contains facts, not myths, *"For we did not follow cleverly devised tales when we made known to you the power and coming of our Lord Jesus Christ, but we were eyewitnesses of His majesty"* (2 Peter 1:16).

I believe the Bible because it is a reliable collection of historical documents written by eyewitnesses. Many others saw with their own eyes, *"What was from the beginning, what we have heard, what we have seen with our eyes, what we have looked at and touched with our hands, concerning the Word of Life— and the life was revealed, and we have seen and testify and proclaim to you the eternal life, which was with the Father and was revealed to us—what we have seen and heard we proclaim to you also, so that you too may have fellowship with us; and indeed our fellowship is with the Father, and with His Son Jesus Christ"* (1 John 1:1-3).

I believe the Bible because it is a reliable collection of historical documents written by eyewitnesses during the lifetime of other eyewitnesses. It was falsifiable because it was written during the lifetime of other eyewitnesses. Had the report been inaccurate, other eyewitnesses could have falsified their claims. When Paul wrote, there were at least 251 eyewitnesses alive who could have falsified his claims had they not been true (1 Corinthians 15:1-4).

More than 25,000 archaeological digs have affirmed and confirmed the validity of the Bible. For the New Testament, there are 6,000 manuscripts dated within 120 years of the original writing. Compare that to other accepted ancient writings. There are only 12 copies of Aristotle's poetics, but they are dated more than 1,000 years afterward. There are only 12 copies of Julius Caesar, and they are dated about 1,000 years afterward. There are 100 copies of Homer's writings, but they are 2,000 years after the original.

Some argue that early scribes intentionally corrupted the Bible. If so, scribes would have needed to corrupt 6,000 manuscripts in three languages (Syriac, Coptic, and Latin) and the commentaries written by early church fathers. They would have had to steal the manuscript copies, change the wording, and replace them without being noticed. Quite absurd. You can trust the Bible!

The Bible is a reliable collection of historical documents written by eyewitnesses during the lifetime of other eyewitnesses who reported supernatural events fulfilling specific prophecies. The Old Testament reported supernatural events (Genesis 1:1-28; Exodus 3:1-6, 14:13-31, 16:4-17). The New Testament also reported supernatural events (Matthew 8:5-13, 9:27-31, 15:32-38, 17:1-8). The fulfillment of prophecy verified the validity that it was of supernatural origin. Isaiah predicted the suffering Savior 700 years prior (Isaiah 53:6-12, Acts 8:26-35). God inspired men to predict the Crucifixion of Jesus 1,000 years before crucifixion was invented (Psalms 22:1, Matthew 27:46).

The Bible is a reliable collection of historical documents written by eyewitnesses during the lifetime of other eyewitnesses who reported supernatural events fulfilling specific prophecies and claimed that their writings were divine rather than human in origin (2 Peter 1:19-21). They spoke what the Lord said (Genesis 15:1; Exodus 9:22; Matthew 2:19, 15:4). They spoke what the Lord said, and it was done.

How can fallible men write an infallible Bible? Fallible men can write an infallible Old Testament when an infallible God superintends the process (Jeremiah 36:2, 4, 17-18, 27, 32). No doubt Jeremiah did and said some stupid things, but God never allowed him to clutter up the Bible with his errors.

And fallible men can write an infallible New Testament when infallible God superintends the process (Ephesians 3:1-7).

Many have heatedly debated the origin of the Bible. Some have said that the natural human mind originated the Bible, while others have argued that a supernatural mind originated it. The Bible itself claims to be a product of the mind of God, *"for no prophecy was ever made by an act of human will, but men moved by the Holy Spirit spoke from God"* (2 Peter 1:21).

**Wisdom contained in Scripture proves that the Bible is of supernatural origin**. The Bible is not written to be a discourse in astronomy. However, its incidental data is sound. Therefore, the wisdom from the astronomy field argues for the Bible's divine origin. Without divine guidance, how could Job have known that there is an empty space in the north? *"He stretches out the north over empty space And hangs the earth on nothing"* (Job 26:7). How would Isaiah know that the earth is a circle? *"It is He who sits above the circle of the earth, And its inhabitants are like grasshoppers, Who stretches out the heavens like a curtain And spreads them out like a tent to live in"* (Isaiah 40:22).

The Bible was not written to be a treaty on biology. However, the incidental biological wisdom in scripture proves that the Bible is of supernatural origin. Many different kinds of animals and plants exist. Some have become extinct. Man is unable to crossbreed any and reproduce the extinct. Why? Because of genetics and heredity laws, each animal and plant produces its kind. Adam knew that from the beginning of creation, *"[11] Then God said, 'Let the earth sprout vegetation, plants yielding seed, and fruit trees on the earth bearing fruit according to their kind with seed in them;' and it was so. [12] The earth produced vegetation, plants yielding seed according to their kind, and trees bearing fruit with seed in them, according to their kind; and God saw that it was good. . . . [21] And God created the great sea creatures and every living creature that moves, with which the waters swarmed, according to their kind, and every winged bird according to its kind; and God saw that it was good. . . . [24] Then God said, "Let the earth produce living creatures according to their kind: livestock and crawling things and animals of the earth according to their kind;' and it was so"* (Genesis 1:11-12, 21, 24).

The Bible was not written as a treaty on medicine. However, the incidental medical wisdom in the Scriptures proves that the Bible is of supernatural origin.

Early medicine did not have the professional status it now enjoys. It was closely identified with pagan religions and superstitions. Illness was attributed to angry gods and evil spirits; therefore, people used mystic rituals to appease the gods and ward off demons thought to cause disease and illnesses.

The germ theory, the principle explaining the cause of infectious disease, evolved in the 19th century. In 1876, a German bacteriologist, Robert Koch, proved that a bacterium caused the disease anthrax. The theory's acceptance led to improved health practices, including quarantine (Leviticus 13:1-6, 8, 34, 52-59).

Humans can live a few weeks without food, a few days without water, but only a few moments without oxygen. Because of hemoglobin, red blood cells carry oxygen to each cell, making life possible. When oxygen-rich blood fails to reach cells, they die. Moses recorded that life was in the blood, *"11 For the life of the flesh is in the blood, and I have given it to you on the altar to make atonement for your souls; for it is the blood by reason of the life that makes atonement. . . . 14 "For as for the life of all flesh, its blood is identified with its life. Therefore, I said to the sons of Israel, 'You are not to eat the blood of any flesh, for the life of all flesh is its blood; whoever eats it shall be cut off"* (Leviticus 17:10-14).

God told Abraham to circumcise newborn males on the eighth day, *"And every male among you who is eight days old shall be circumcised throughout your generations, including a slave who is born in the house or who is bought with money from any foreigner, who is not of your descendants"* (Genesis 17:12). Why the eighth day?

In 1935, Professor H. Dam discovered "vitamin K," a factor in foods that helped prevent hemorrhage in baby chicks. We now know that Vitamin K is responsible for the liver's production of prothrombin. A prothrombin deficiency will occur if vitamin K is deficient, and hemorrhagic may occur. Oddly enough, vitamin K begins to be produced only on the 5th through the 7th days of the newborn male's life (the vitamin is usually produced by bacteria in the intestinal tract). It is only on the eighth day of the entire life of the newborn that the blood clotting element prothrombin is above 100%. The best day for circumcision is, therefore, the eighth day. But how did Abraham know with his limited scientific knowledge?

The Bible was not written to be a treaty on oceanography. However, the incidental oceanographic wisdom in Scripture proves that the Bible is of supernatural origin.

When running at average speed, the Mississippi River dumps approximately 6,052,500 gallons of water per second into the Gulf of Mexico. Where does the water go? The Gulf never overflows. This wisdom was contained in the Bible long before the scientific discovery, *"All the rivers flow into the sea, Yet the sea is not full . . ."* (Ecclesiastes 1:7).

Before scientific discovery, the Bible reported the hydrologic cycle: *"If the clouds are full, they pour out rain on the earth; . . . "* (Ecclesiastes 11:3). Evaporation takes water away from the earth, filling the clouds. Condensation empties the clouds, returning the water to the earth as rain, snow, hail, or sleet (Amos 9:6).

It is not the intelligent man who says I cannot believe the Bible; it is the fool. The intelligent man believes the Bible. Many scholars have endeavored to disprove the Bible's accuracy. They have all failed. It has been proven that the Bible is archaeologically, historically, and scientifically true. That's why I choose to believe the Bible!

# CREATION VS. EVOLUTION

*"In the beginning God created the heavens and the earth."*
Genesis 1:1

**CREATION vs. EVOLUTION**
Everyone knows that Christianity is a religion. Religion is just a set of beliefs that governs rituals and routines. The Christian religion is a set of beliefs concerning the universe's cause, nature, and purpose. Fundamental Christianity rests on the foundation that a Self-Sustaining God supernaturally created the universe and sent His only begotten Son into the world to solve the sin problem.

Unfortunately, atheists [those who say there is enough evidence to know that there is *no* God] and agnostics [those who say there is *not* enough evidence to know that there is a God] have ridiculed its basic beliefs for centuries. They have great difficulty believing in a supernatural creator.

Few people understand that evolution is a religion, too. The proponents of evolution have perpetrated one of the biggest lies and con jobs on humanity ever in human history – that evolution is science and not a religion.

Atheists ask, where did God come from? Christians say we do not know … but believe … thus making it a faith religion. Christians ask, where did energy, matter, and space come from? Atheists say we do not know … but we believe … thus making it a faith religion. Since both are faith religions, which requires more faith: to believe that God created or that nothing created?

"Science" comes from the Latin "Scientia," meaning knowledge. How do we define science? According to Webster's New Collegiate Dictionary, the definition of science is "knowledge attained through study or practice" or "knowledge covering general truths of the operation of general laws, esp. as obtained and tested through scientific method [and] concerned with the physical world."

What does that mean? Science refers to a system of acquiring knowledge. This system uses observation and experimentation to describe and explain natural phenomena. The term "science" also refers to the organized body of knowledge people have gained using that system.

But do you realize what evolution truly is, stated in utmost simplicity?

> (A) Here is the evolutionary formula for making a universe: Nothing + nothing = two elements + time = 92 natural elements + time = all physical laws and a completely structured universe of galaxies, systems, stars, planets, and moons orbiting in perfect balance and order. Even then it takes faith to believe that nothing + nothing = two elements when there is no science, observation, and experimentation to support the claim.
>
> (B) Here is the evolutionary formula for making life: Dirt + water + time = living creatures.

Belief in these formulas requires an unimaginable faith. This faith constitutes a religion. Unfortunately, this religion is based upon an unsubstantiated faith.

There are three essential areas into which evolution cannot move or solve. It cannot bridge the gap: (1) from nothing to something, (2) from something to life, and (3) between life and humanity. The idea of life beginning spontaneously is an absolute matter of faith on the part of the biologist.

## The Creation

After many excavations in the Middle East, archaeologists have found ancient writings called "cuneiform" writings that date back to 3500 B.C. Since Adam was still alive then, writing could have gone back even further. Adam could have composed an account of creation. Could Moses take the **earlier documents of Adam, Noah, Abraham, Enoch, Isaac, and Jacob**, which were passed on from one generation to the next, and put them together into one book called the Book of Genesis?

It may be a surprise to some people, but writing is mentioned in Genesis 5:1, which says, "This is the **book** of the generations of Adam." This suggests that the art of writing was known within Adam's lifetime, which could make writing as old as humans themselves! Cuneiform writing became the system used by all civilized countries east of the Mediterranean-Assyrian,

Babylonia, Persia, and the Hittites. Cuneiform writing consists of wedge-shaped impressions made in plastic clay. The Hebrew word for "to write" means "to cut in" or "to dig." Abraham, Isaac, and Jacob would have used this system of writing.

Although papyrus was the common writing material in Egypt, Cuneiform writing was understood as the Tell-el-Amarna tablets found in Egypt in 1888 reveal. Among these clay tablets were letters, dated about 1400 B.C., from Palestinian officials to the Egyptian government- all written in Cuneiform.

It is no wonder that God allowed Pharaoh's daughter to raise Moses. He could have quickly learned cuneiform writing so he could translate the Hebrew Cuneiform tablets of Abraham, Isaac, Jacob, Noah, and Adam for the Israelites in the wilderness. Even in the book of Acts, in chapter 7 verses 21-22, Stephen says: *"And after he had been set outside, Pharaoh's daughter took him away and nurtured him as her own son. Moses was educated in all the learning of the Egyptians, and he was a man of power in words and deeds."*

Creationists argue that God created the universe, including both and living matter. In the book of Genesis, God recorded the history of humans' beginnings.

The book of Genesis contains the history of the beginning of Creation. God began the Creation by issuing "ten commandments." Ten times in Genesis chapter one, God said, "Let" (Genesis 1:3; 6; 9; 11; 14; 20; 24; 26; 28; 29). He spoke the universe into existence.

Jesus Christ authenticated the biblical record of the history of the Creation (Matthew 19:3-4; Mark 10:6; 13:19). Jesus knew about the Creation because He participated in the Creation (Colossians 1:16-19; Genesis 1:26).

The book of Genesis contains the history of the continuation of the Creation. God continued the Creation by issuing "ten commandments." Ten times in Genesis chapter one it is recorded that God said, "After their kind" (11; 12; 12; 21; 21; 24; 24; 25; 25; 25). He spoke the continuation of the universe into existence.

This book of Genesis contains the history of Creation. Life came only from life (Genesis 1:11a). Even now, life only comes from like life (Genesis 1:11b). There may be mutations within a given "kind," but there is no transmutation between different "kinds."

A mutation is a permanent change in a gene's DNA sequence. Mutations in a gene's DNA sequence can alter the amino acid sequence of the protein encoded by the gene.

How does this happen? Like words in a sentence, the DNA sequence of each gene determines the amino acid sequence for the protein it encodes. The DNA sequence is interpreted in groups of three nucleotide bases called codons. Each codon specifies a single amino acid in a protein.
We can think about the DNA sequence of a gene as a sentence made up entirely of three-letter words. In the sequence, each three-letter word is a codon, specifying a single amino acid in a protein. Have a look at this sentence:

Thesunwashotbuttheoldmandidnotgethishat.

If you were to split this sentence into individual three-letter words, you would probably read it like this:

The sun was hot but the old man dic not get his hat.

This sentence represents a gene. Each letter corresponds to a nucleotide base, and each word represents a codon. What if you shifted the three-letter "reading frame?" You would end up with

T hes unw ash otb utt heo ldm and idn otg eth ish at.

Or

Th esu nwa sho tbu tth eol dma ndi dno tge thi sha t.

The fact that God created [issued 10 commands] the universe kills evolution dead in its tracks. The fact of how God continues [issued 10 commands] the universe fatally seals the coffin of evolution.
God created this universe. He created living and non-living matter. The book of Genesis contains the history of the beginning of the Creation. After placing the peripheral of the universe in position, God began the next phase of Creation by issuing "ten commandments." Ten times, God said, "Let" (Genesis 1:3; 6; 9; 11; 14; 20; 24; 26; 28; 29). He spoke the universe into existence.

Several thousand years later, Jesus Christ authenticated the biblical record of the history of the Creation. When some Pharisees questioned Him about marriage, He referred them to the order of marriage from Creation, "And He answered and said, "Have you not read that He who created them from *the beginning made them male and female"* (Matthew 19:3-4; Mark 10:6; 13:19). Jesus knew about the Creation because He participated in the Creation. God created all things through Jesus and for Jesus (Colossians 1:16-19).

The book of Genesis contains the history of the continuation of Creation. God continued Creation by issuing another "ten commandments." Ten times in Genesis chapter one, God said, "After their kind" (11; 12; 12; 21; 24; 25). He spoke the continuation of the universe into existence.

According to the theory of evolution, there is no first cause, uncaused, or superintending intelligence, nor divine guidance of any kind that has caused the universe and its inhabitants to be as they are. All that exists does so because of a meandering, blind, chance that has taken place over eons of time.

### The General Theory of Evolution or Organic Evolution

Please carefully investigate the definitions of evolution by these able scientists.

"On the other hand, there is the theory that all the living forms in the world have risen from a single source which itself came from an inorganic form. This theory can be called the General Theory of Evolution." **Dr. George A. Kerkut, *The Implications of Evolution*, Pergamon Press, London, 1960, p.157.**

"Evolution is a fully natural process, inherent in the physical properties of the universe, by which life arose in the first place and by which all living things, past or present, have since developed, divergently and progressively." **Dr. George G. Simpson, *Science,* April 1, 1960, p. 969.**

### The Special Theory of Evolution

"Things can and do change, but those changes always take place within very narrow, very restricted limits." Crossbreeding produces this kind of evolution. This kind of evolution is always restricted to the "kind" that produced it (Genesis 1:11, 12, 21, 24, 25). There is no controversy over this theory of evolution. Both evolutionists and creationists accept this theory to be valid.

Life only comes from life therefore life came only from life: Then God said, *"Let the earth sprout vegetation, plants yielding seed, and fruits trees on the earth..."* (Genesis 1:11a). Even now life only comes from "like" life, *"... bearing fruit after their kind with seed in them..."* (Genesis 1:11b). The fact that God created the universe kills evolution dead in its tracks. The fact of how God continues the universe fatally seals the coffin of evolution. It is now time, once and for all, to bury the lie of the general theory of evolution.

The evidence overrules the objections to the proposition that God created the universe. The Creation speaks volumes about God. The Creation says that God is powerful. The created universe never needs repair. No wonder God aggressively interrogated Job (Job 38:1-15). The creation of the materials of the universe demonstrates His power (Acts 17:24). Where did the power to bring the universe into existence come? It came from God Himself!

The creation of the immaterial of the universe demonstrates His power. God created condensation and evaporation (Amos 9:6, 5:8), gravity (Colossians 1:16-17), and even the concept of forgiveness (Ephesians 4:32). Indeed, forgiveness is a novel idea.

The Creation says that God is not only powerful but wise (1 Corinthians 2:6-9). The order of Creation demonstrates His wisdom. First, God created plants and then animals. Animals needed plants for food. Yet, for pollination, some plants needed animals (bees) to survive. A day could not have been a long period of time; if so, all plants would have died.

The organism of Creation demonstrates His wisdom. The organism of the family and its unity argues for the wisdom of God (Ephesians 5:22-6:4). The organism of the church and its unity argues for the wisdom of God (Ephesians 1:20-23, 2:12-22, 3:1-6, 5:32-33).

 **GOD**

**God-The First Cause (cosmological)**
The Athenians believed in, named, and provided statues for the gods they had named. Just in case there existed a god that they were unaware of, they provided an extra statue designating it for the "unknown god." When the apostle Paul saw their ignorance, he proceeded to inform them of the one God who really was unknown to them (Acts 17:22-31). He persuaded some, others he did not persuade (Acts 17:32-34).

The existence of God has been placed on trial. Many have asked, "If God exists then why do disease, disaster, and death continually devastate the innocent?" This question has caused many to doubt the existence of God.

We build all our life upon the foundation of probabilities. Probability is the ratio of occurrences to non-occurrences. Probability is the percentage of assurance that something will occur, but it always falls somewhere less than 100% of absolute certainty. Within the human realm, there are no 100% absolute certainties.

There is never a 100% absolute certainty that the airplane will safely reach its destination. However, there is a greater probability that it will than that it will not. Therefore, with confidence we make reservations, purchase our tickets, and board saying, "I will call you when I get there."

There is a greater probability that God exists than that He does not. Who put this universe here? The sun, moon, and stars are included in the universe. The existence of the sun, moon, and stars forces us to proclaim that, "someone put them here!" Who is that Someone?

Someone caused the universe to exist. All that exists is caused by someone who existed prior to the existence of what was created. This forces us retrospectively to an "uncaused cause" raising the probability that God exists.

This is what historians call the **"Cosmological Argument"** for the existence of the universe. Cosmo means "world" and logos means "reason." Therefore, this argument puts forth a reason for the existence of the world, *"The God who made the world and everything that is in it, since He is Lord of heaven and earth, does not dwell in temples made by hands"* (Acts 17:24; Genesis 1:1-31).

Who put life here? Plants, animals, and human beings are alive. Living plants, animals and human beings force us to proclaim, "someone put life here!" Some living one has caused life to exist. All that lives is caused by someone who lived prior. This forces us retrospectively to a living uncaused cause. Even if there was a big bang, I ask, "Who pulled the trigger?" Someone had to rig the trigger and then pull the trigger. Challenge those who disbelieve in the existence of God. Ask them who put it (the universe) here?

**God-The First Designer (teleological)**
Who put this universe here like this? The sun, moon, and stars are arranged according to design. When we observe the arranged design of the sun, moon, and stars, we are forced to proclaim, "Someone put them here like this!" Someone caused the universe to exist like this. Design requires a designer that existed prior to the time of the design. This forces us retrospectively to an "uncaused cause designer."

This is what historians call the **"Teleological Argument."** The cosmological argument looks at the universe and sees "cause," while the teleological argument looks at the universe and sees "design." That designed complexity of the universe forces us to proclaim: "Some One designed it like this" (Genesis 1:11, 14-19, 21-30; Job 26:7-10; Psalms 104:19; 139:14; Isaiah 40:22; Amos 5:8, 9:6; Acts 17:26; 1 Corinthians 15:40-41).

Who put this life here like this? Plants, animals, and human beings radiate intelligent design. The intelligent design forces us to proclaim: "Someone put them here like this!" Someone caused life to exist like this. All intelligent design is caused by a designer that existed before the existence of that which was created. This forces us retrospectively to an uncaused cause designer of life. Even if there was a big bang, I ask, "Who pointed it in the designed direction in which it fired?" Challenge those who disbelieve. Ask them who put it (the universe) here like this.

The rotating, revolving synchronization of the sun, moon, earth, and stars argues for intelligent design. The synchronization of the complexities of life argues for intelligent design. Intelligent design constantly argues for an intelligent designer.

The creation worldview sees God as the creator Who, through supernatural processes, is responsible for the origin, sustaining, and governing of the universe and all that is within it. This worldview is the basis for Christianity.

For the Creationist, there are absolutes. Hence, there is an objective truth. Within this Creationist worldview, the apostle Paul argued for objective truth (Romans 1:18-19, 25, 28, 32).

From the first to the last scripture, God reveals Himself as the One and only true God, beside whom there is no other (Deuteronomy 6:5; Isaiah 43:10; James 2:19). What is essential is that we readily confess all that scripture affirms about God. However, we do not need answers, for they do not help. We need a relationship with God: That is what helps!

# MORALITY VS NO MORALITY

**MORALITY VS NO MORALITY**
For the Creationist, there are moral absolutes. There are expressions of moral absolutes of right and wrong, wherein all are accountable (Romans 1:24-32). They would argue that thriving families and societies depend on morality.

For the Creationist, there are (1) absolutes, objective truths, (2) moral absolutes, expressions that are right and wrong, of which all are accountable, and (3) moral absolute values. Value is an individual's sense of moral worth and/or significance assigned to or derived from achieving a goal or standard. It is the prized priority that a person places upon something or someone. For example, to give a charitable gift to a person in need adds worth and significance to the one who gives and receives (Acts 2:40-47; 2 Corinthians 8:1-5). Values affect our decisions, which in turn affect our behavior. When our values are moral, we may recommend them to others (Romans 1:32).

There are (1) self-values - self-concept, esteem, worth, confidence (ex) feeling good about yourself, (2) preference values - likes vs. dislikes these are more subjective (ex) like coke, dislike Pepsi, (3) conduct values - guidelines, principles, standards, ethics (ex) lying is wrong, (4) cultural values - a shared set of ideas or beliefs for a part of a group (ex) religion, and (5) cognitive values - objective evidence (ex) consumer reports, researched values.

For the Evolutionist, there are no moral absolutes. Though some claim to be moral but the foundation for their morality fluctuates. There are no expressions of moral absolutes of right and wrong, wherein all are accountable (Romans 1:24-32). They would argue that thriving families and societies do not depend on morality.

For the evolutionist, there are no (1) absolutes, objective truths, only subjective truths; (2) moral absolutes, expressions that are right and wrong of which all are accountable; and (3) moral absolute values. There is no moral worth and/or significance assigned to or derived from achieving a goal or standard. One should never recommend their value to another (Romans 1:32; 1 John 3:17).

For the evolutionist, nothing has value unless one decides to assign value. We can be as cruel as nature, the "survival of the fittest."

Morality is defined as a code of ethics to which all are accountable. It is right and wrong behavior that either sustains or destroys peace between (1) an individual and his/her creator, (2) an individual and him/herself, or (3) an individual and another individual or groups of individuals. Many rejected the Creator God as the source of their standard of morality (Romans 1:21, 25, 28). Their rebellious attitude gave rise to their evolutionary thinking. Evolutionary thinking created chaos in our world.

Is there one thing that each person believes is right or wrong? If the conduct of an individual or society can be genuinely criticized, we must then have an objective standard by which to critique conduct. We call that reference point of right and wrong morality. If there is a standard of morality, then there must be a source who assigns moral rules. Morality does exist. There is a source who assigns moral rules. Through written scripture, God provides the best standard for morality. What other standards have some chosen?

Some have chosen intuition as their standard for morality. Intuition is the principle of instantaneous thought without clear reasoning being the foremost and final authority for determining what is right and wrong behavior. Some believe that people automatically know what is right and wrong. If intuition is the source, one could never critique the conduct of another. We could not account for differences of opinion between two focused individuals. Individuals would never have a conscience burden for wrong choices, even when the result indicated a wrong choice had been made. Intuition may be a factor but it falls far short of acceptability (Jeremiah 10:23; Judges 21:25; Proverbs 12:15; 14:12; 16:25; Acts 26:9-18; Romans 14:5).

Some have chosen consequentialism as their standard for morality. Consequentialism is the principle of the ultimate outcome being the foremost and final authority for determining what is right and wrong behavior. Usually, we can never know the ultimate outcome. We may be unable to determine the consequences until after a course of behavior had been followed. Therefore, in many instances, we would not know until it was too late. Consequences may be a factor, but consequences fall far short alone (1 Samuel 15:1-24; Romans 6:21; 2 Thessalonians 3:10).

Some have chosen society as their standard of morality. Society is the principle of the majority being the foremost and final authority for determining right and wrong behavior. How do we determine the majority? Is it country, county, or community? Is it geographical, economical, or cultural?
What do you do when two or more societies differ? For 444 days, the Iranians held 52 Americans hostage. The majority within that society approved. How can we Americans criticize their behavior? Society may be considered (Acts 16:3; Galatians 2:3), but society falls far short.

Through written scripture, God provides the best standard for our morality. In every aspect, biblical principles are economically, physiologically, and psychologically sound. God wants us to recommend the Bible as the best standard for morality.

## Character

Character is the willingness to do right. Amid the mountain of gray areas, there is still some black and white. Some "rights" and some "wrongs" remain.

Character is the willingness to do right as God defines it. As the Law Giver, God exercises divine authority and administrative ownership over everything that exists or has ever existed (Exodus 4:10-13; Isaiah 6:1, 8, 11). He, Himself, absolutely establishes the standard of right and wrong. When consequentialism, majority rule, and intuition have exhausted their finiteness, morality positions itself upon the shoulders of God Almighty.

Not only is there a Law Giver, but there is also a Law given. When all has been said about grace, a Law is given (Romans 7:22-25) that shows us what we should be. The Holy Spirit pushes us to be what we can be, while Jesus Christ shows us what we will be. We must submit to rules we did not vote on because there is a system of right and wrong for which we had no input. Therefore, we must develop the will to do what is right as God defines right.

Character is the willingness to do right, as God defines it, because that is what we should do. Character also causes us to do right, as God defines it, for instrumental reasons. A significant degree of good is done, and damage is prevented by doing right. Shadrach, Meshach, and Abed-nego declared that they would serve God, for they believed that God could deliver them (Daniel 3:15-17). They anticipated some good would result from their steadfast allegiance to their God, yet there is more.

For intrinsic reasons, character causes us to do right, as God defines right. The human mind is often incapable of perceiving much of the good that results from our obedience to God. Obedience allows us to escape a guilty conscience, but we must commit to maintaining our character. Others before us have, as will others after us.

Shadrach, Meshach and Abed-nego declared they would serve God even if He did not deliver them (Daniel 3:13-18). They would do right just because it was right to do so. God is always right, and He made us in His image. Therefore, He wants us to do what is right because it reflects His nature.

However, doing right does not always produce a noticeable benefit. Sometimes, we must do right to maintain our character. Not only does the apparent benefit often escape our notice, but there may also occasionally be a cost of doing right. Nevertheless, character demands that we do what is right because it is right, regardless of the cost.

## The Atheists

Atheists refuse to acknowledge the existence of God. They say, "We do know that God does not exist" (Psalms 14:1). Despite the evidence of His existence, they claim to know that there is no God (Romans 1:20). Frequently, they say, "If God exists, He would instantly and completely eliminate all evil from the earth." I ask, "Who would remain if God instantly removed all evil?" No one, not even the person who alleges such, for all are evil (Romans 3:9-18).

God is eliminating evil. He is progressively removing evil. Through the hearts of human beings, God is eliminating evil (Acts 17:30; 2 Corinthians 5:17-20; James 5:19-20; Ephesians 2:11-22; Galatians 4:4). God seeks to destroy evil, one heart at a time.

## The Agnostics

Agnostics refuse to acknowledge the existence of God. They say, "We do not know that God does exist" (Psalms 19:1-11). Despite the evidence of His existence, they claim not to know that God does exist (Romans 1:19). Frequently, they say, "If God exists, He would instantly and completely eliminate all human suffering from the earth." I ask, "Why is there human suffering on the earth?" Human suffering stems from sin (evil) on earth, and even the sin of the person who alleges such has caused some human suffering (Romans 8:18-25).

God is eliminating human suffering. He is progressively removing human suffering. Through the hearts of human beings, God is eliminating human suffering (12 Corinthians 1:3-7).

Let God be the God that they want Him to be. Allow Him to eliminate evil, admitting that ultimately, He will destroy all evil. Allow Him to eradicate human suffering, acknowledging that ultimately, He will eliminate all evil human suffering.

He can't eliminate all suffering until He eliminates all sin. He can't eliminate all sin until He eliminates all sinners. Progressively, He eliminates sinners when they are born again, but ultimately, He will eliminate sinners when they are destroyed.

# SECTION 3

# SHARE INTELLECTUAL WISDOM

# GATHERING INFORMATION

**GATHERING INFORMATION**

What will happen to your gathered wisdom when you die? Unless you deposit it into the hearts of others who remain, it will smother into the dust of the cemetery with you. You have an excellent opportunity to plant all your wisdom so that it continues to live and grow. I will challenge you to do so and even coach you on how to do it. You may leave it verbally or leave it visually (writing).

**William Glasser (psychologist) said that we learn ...**
1) 10% of what we read.
2) 20% of what we hear.
3) 30% of what we see.
4) 50% of what we see and hear.
5) 70% of what we discuss with others.
6) 80% of what we experience personally.
7) 95% of what we teach others.

Through teaching, you help students organize information, enabling them to grasp it consciously and conscientiously apply it.

Teaching requires one to study. Teach everything that you learn to your younger siblings. If you have no siblings available, teach other children. Teaching reinforces your learning. Your teaching enables other children.

Look at the letters below. See if you can memorize them in ten (10) seconds.
T hes unw ash otb utt heo ldm and idn otg eth ish at.

Look at the letters below. See if you can memorize them in ten (10) seconds.
Th esu nwa sho tbu tth eol dma ndi dno tge thi sha t.

Look at the letters below. See if you can memorize them in ten (10) seconds.
Thesunwashotbuttheoldmandidnotgethishat.

Look at the letters below. See if you can memorize them in ten (10) seconds.
The sun was hot but the old man did not get his hat.

The parameters in which you place information (letters) greatly increase the comprehension rate of your students.

# WRITING

If you are writing for a class project, clarify instructions from your instructor before you begin to write. Decide on your objective before you start to write. Craft a concise propositional statement of seventeen words or less. Write 7-11 questions that your article should answer.

**Search for Information**

Use your local library's website to access electronic resources. Some libraries have special access to journal articles. You can also talk to a librarian in the reference section about your research topic. Google Scholar can also be very helpful.

In addition to published books, search scholarly and professional journals for peer-reviewed articles. Studious researchers and well-trained practitioners within a particular discipline will usually write these articles.

Peer review is a well-accepted indicator of quality scholarship. It is the process by which an author's peers read a paper submitted for publication. Several recognized researchers will evaluate a manuscript and recommend its publication, revision, or rejection. Articles accepted for publication through a peer review process implicitly meet the discipline's expected standards of expertise.

Articles in some scholarly and professional journals are not peer-reviewed but are selected by an editor or board. Standards of scholarship in such journals are often equal or comparable to those of peer-reviewed publications, although this is not always the case.

Also, search for information in the "study of studies." Researchers, independently of each other, will research and write the results of their studies. Another researcher may then study the studies that several researchers have already done. From his study, he will write a summation of what he discovered from studying the studies. This study of studies is likely the purest research available.

## Select Information

Books or articles you read for research must be used and discarded quickly. You need information. The source you are reading has information. The problem is that it has too much information irrelevant to your research topic. Skillfully sift quickly through the material you don't need, find the material you do need, and abandon the rest.

Look at the title page, preface, foreword, and introduction. Check out the table of contents and look at the index. Watch for key propositions. A fundamental proposition is a statement of the author's beliefs. Carefully check out the author's conclusion at the end of the article.

Give the book a run-through, reading the opening and concluding portions of each chapter, considering the subheadings in the body of each chapter, going over any summary or conclusion chapter at the end of the book, and possibly looking up a book review or two if the book is confusing or potentially controversial.

## Organize Information

Write each major idea on a separate sheet of paper or index card. Read your research materials. Whenever you read information pertaining to your propositional statement, write it under the main idea where it fits.

When you finish reading and writing, organize the information into your paper. Arrange information according to your outline. Remove redundant information that does not add to the emphasis of your writing. Read more articles if you need more information to sufficiently produce the writing. As you read and edit, you may decide to make even significant changes. Do not hesitate to change your propositional statement and/or your outline if the researched information demands it.

## Words

Remove weak and overused words such as: "just," "really," "very," "perhaps/maybe," "quite," "amazing," "literally," "stuff," "things," and "got." Verbs are the power words. Select them strategically.

## Structure

Develop an outline by thinking in terms of the introduction, body, and ending of the book. Write the book that you want to read.

## Argumentation

Academic and professional writing must make an argument. An argument makes a claim intended to solve a problem by giving others a good reason to structure their beliefs and behaviors. Your argument must provide rational reasons for your recommended preferences.

These five questions form the basis for an argument:

1. What do you think? What's your point? What are you claiming that I should do or believe?

2. Why do you think that? Why should I agree? What reasons can you offer to support your claim?

3. How do you know? On what facts do you base those reasons? How do we know they are good reasons? What evidence do you have to back them up? We consider reasons, but evidence must be found within the text or source.

4. What's your logic? What principle makes your reasons relevant to your claim? We'll call that principle a warrant.

5. Anticipate these pushbacks. But have you considered it? But what would you say to someone who said/objected/argued/ claimed? Do you acknowledge this alternative to your position, and how would you respond?

Writing allows you to deliberately capture details and contour them into a skillfully orchestrated presentation. Writing allows for a most potent and provocative presentation.

## Structuring Propositions

Develop your propositional statement. The thesis statement is one clear sentence of what you will tell or attempt to tell the reader. This must be a simple sentence, preferably 17 words or less.

You may state the proposition in a variety of ways. Your objective

for the writing will dictate how you will state the proposition. Below are six different propositions:
1) *a possibility proposition*: You can learn Spanish.
2) *a predictive proposition*: You will learn Spanish in three months.
3) *a persuasive proposition*: You ought to learn Spanish.
4) *an evaluative proposition*: Learning Spanish is easier than learning English.
5) *a declarative proposition*: Knowing Spanish opens career opportunities.
6) *a comparative proposition*: Learning Spanish is different from learning German.

Questioning the proposition provides an outline of the structure of the lesson. The structure is just organized thinking.

Frequently used questions are "What," "Why," "How," "Who," "When," "Which," and "Where."

Asking "what" leads to further knowledge.

Asking "why" leads to motivation.

Asking "how" leads to procedures.

A typical expository (or argumentative) essay consists of an introduction, a body, and a conclusion. The introduction contains the thesis statement, which is a sentence that explains the idea that the writer will support (or argue for) in his essay. The thesis statement must be a simple sentence, usually of 17 words or less.

The introductory paragraph contains general points or attention-grabbing details leading to the main idea. These hooks may be an amusing or interesting anecdote, a question, a quotation, and a startling or paradoxical statement.

The body of the paragraph often begins with a transition word or words like "First" or "The first of these reasons" and gives examples and/or details relating to the first supporting reason. The next or later paragraphs may begin with a transition word or words like "Next" or "Second" or "Another reason" or "The second of these reasons" and give examples and/or details relating to the second supporting reason.

The paragraph that concludes the body often begins with a transition word or words like "Finally," "Last," or "The final reason" and gives examples and/or details relating to the third supporting reason (which is often the strongest of the three).

The conclusion paragraph may begin with "In conclusion," "To conclude," or "Clearly" and often restates the thesis statement in different words. It may move from there to a general comment about life, a final important point, or a suggestion about future action that may be needed. Influential writings often end with a relevant quotation, question, prediction, or warning.

Begin your rough draft. Ensure that every sentence directly relates to your assigned topic (as stated in your thesis statement). If you can't think of the right word or phrase, leave a blank space (circle it) and return when you have finished your rough copy. Don't look up words in a dictionary or thesaurus at this stage. Circle words you may want to change and come back to them when you've finished your rough copy.

When you've finished your rough copy, revise and edit it by adding, deleting, rearranging, and substituting material (use a dictionary and a thesaurus). As well as correct errors in spelling, capitalization, punctuation, subject-verb agreement, verb tense consistency, and pronoun agreement.

Regarding unity: Is my essay unified? Do all parts contribute to the main idea, and have I avoided digression? Have I supported all generalizations that I made? Have I given enough emphasis to each part of my essay?

Regarding structure: Is my introduction interesting? Will it catch the reader's interest? Does my thesis statement delineate my assigned subject? Does my conclusion give a sense of finality or completion?

Regarding paragraphing and transition: Does the first sentence of each paragraph provide an idea about what each paragraph discusses? Has each sentence been developed properly, using one or more methods for developing paragraphs: examples, details, reasons, comparison/contrast, cause, effect, etc.? Does each sentence relate directly to the purpose of the paper as stated in the thesis statement? Is there a clear transition from the last sentence of each paragraph to the first sentence of the next paragraph? Have I used adequate transitional words or phrases?

Regarding coherence: Have I used adequate transitional words and phrases to connect the sentences so that they flow smoothly from one to the next and are coherent (i.e., "stuck together" or connected)?

Regarding sentences: Have I used mainly complex (rather than superficial) sentences and used a variety of different sentence lengths?

Regarding diction: Have I removed all slang, jargon, and unnecessary clichés from my diction? Is my vocabulary vibrantly adequate for the culture of the presentation? Remember that verbs are your power words, not adjectives and adverbs.

Regarding footnoting and bibliography: Have I introduced and handled quotations properly and acknowledged accurately in footnotes and in a proper bibliography everything that requires acknowledgment? Note: A good style text that covers footnoting and creates a bibliography is an essential tool for the essay writer.

## Essays

Follow the aforementioned writing techniques. Carefully read your assigned essay topic to determine exactly what it is that you are supposed to be discussing in your paper. Limit your essay topic to a manageable size and formulate an effective thesis statement that is to be the main idea or central focus of your paper. This statement is very often a generalization that prepares readers for the supporting details that follow.

Brainstorm for ideas that support your thesis statement. Organize your ideas into an outline, keeping in mind the method of paragraph development (e.g., details, examples, reasons, cause and effect, comparison and contrast, etc.) that you wish to employ. Before you agonize over developing your outline, remember that an outline is the organized thinking that answers questions about the proposition. The outline will be major points and sub-points that are the ideas that fit under your propositional statement.

An essay may have multiple purposes. But besides it all, you are writing to argue for a particular point of view or to explain the steps necessary to complete a task.

1. Research. Research your topic. Make wise use of the wisdom of great thinkers.
2. Analyze. Detail the evidence and research from their claims.
3. Brainstorm. Ask and answer the questions that are within your mind. Think through others' thoughts until you have original insights.
4. Proposition. Develop your propositional statement into one clear sentence of what you are going to tell or attempt to tell the reader. This must be a simple sentence, preferably 17 words or less.
5. Outline. Describe paragraphs using one-line sentences.
6. Introduction. The introduction expands the proposition by telling the audience what the essay will argue.
7. Paragraphs. Each paragraph should focus on a single idea that supports your proposition.
8. Conclusion. Wrap up the writing in such a manner that the reader walks away with something memorable.

**Term Papers**

Follow the aforementioned writing techniques. Carefully read your assigned essay topic to determine exactly what it is that you are supposed to be discussing in your paper. Limit your essay topic to a manageable size and formulate an effective thesis statement that is to be the main idea or central focus of your paper. This statement is very often a generalization that prepares readers for the supporting details that follow.

Brainstorm for ideas that support your thesis statement. Organize your ideas into an outline, keeping in mind the method of paragraph development (e.g., details, examples, reasons, cause and effect, comparison and contrast, etc.) that you wish to employ. Before you agonize over developing your outline, remember that an outline is the organized thinking that answers questions about the proposition. The outline will be major points and sub-points that are the ideas that fit under your propositional statement.

# PUBLISHING

**Book - General**

Develop your writing skills and techniques. Improve your grammar. Attend writing seminars and network with other authors. Learn practical techniques to stimulate your imagination and innovative thinking. Find inspiration in the world around you. Get over creative fear blocks.

Start small. Have a set time to write each day. Remain accountable to your writing process. Stay motivated and get early feedback. Embrace failure and write another book. Think in terms of 10,000-word increments and break each chapter into roughly equal lengths.

Get started and get there. Visualize thousands of people reading and recommending your book (writing) for others to read. You do not have to pause your life to write. In four months, writing two pages per day, you can write a one-hundred-and-twenty-page book.

The writing mechanics for a book include the mechanics for writing an essay or term paper. With the essay or term paper, your instructor will, to some degree, decide the direction of your writing. But with your book, you will exercise exclusive jurisdiction. You write the essay or term paper for academic credit. You write your book to tell your story and to make a financial profit.

Therefore, in the book, you must capture the interest of the reader by starting with an interesting idea, need or relevant topic. Introduce the topic, make a claim, express an opinion, or ask a pertinent question.

Develop the body of the book. Use the mechanics of writing the essay or term paper to write the body. Just write, and write, and write; you can edit later. You can decide the chapters as you begin, or you can decide them near the end of the writing.

State your conclusion. Show how your conclusion logically proceeds from the body of information that you have provided.

## Book – Specific

Your life's exposures, experiences and interpretations contain therapeutic and redemptive value. When they are collected in a book, they start living in the lives of others throughout eternity.

Through writing, you can safely tell your story. Your peers will greatly respect and admire you when they read your polished publication. And the purchasing public will provide you with an additional stream of income.

## My Journey

In 1991, in my master's degree program at Memphis State University, now the University at Memphis, I wrote a research paper ***"Single Parenting Stimulates A Positive Family Networking Among Black Families."*** The University selected my research paper as one of three papers to be presented at the Graduate Research Symposium. Ph.D. students who were completing their doctoral studies wrote the other two research papers.

Yet, I still needed a kick in the seat of the pants and a coaching mentor. Dr. Kenneth Gilmore, Sr. served as my writing mentor. For years, he coerced and coached me to write. After much agony, I reluctantly began.

## Good And Angry

I published my first book, *Good And Angry – Your Personal Gide to Anger Management*, in 2003. It is a strong seller even today, after being on the market for 20 years.

Since then, I have written 19 more. Each one has become financially profitable within an average of 12 months.

You have been thinking about writing a book? I have successfully written and published many books. Also, I have coached several to successfully write and publish their book.

## ▶ Module #1 ~ Pre-writing

Everything has a starting point. Writing your book is no different. You must start at a point of origination and proceed to a point of the destination. Fortunately for you, my many years of writing and numerous publications have provided experience that will expedite your writing program. Now let's start here:

1) Read the book: *Elements of Style* by William Strunk, Jr. and E. B. White.

2) Read the book: *Mastering the Craft of Writing* by Stephen Wilbers.

3) Read four good books (1 per week). Note what makes them good.

4) Build up your beliefs and begin formulating your ideas.

5) Ask yourself these questions:

    a. Why am I writing this book?

    b. What am I passionate about?

    c. What skills have I mastered?

    d. What stories will I share?

    e. What exposures will I share?

    f. What experiences will I share?

    g. What interpretations will I share?

    h. What is my book about?

    i. Is it personal, subjective experiences?

    j. Is it researched, objective documentation?

k.  What is the genre, class, or category of my book?

l.  Who is my target audience?

m.  What is their attention span?

n.  What are their key interests?

o.  What problem can I solve?

p.  What problems can I create by forcing people to think outside the norm?

q.  What common questions of my target audience will my book answer?

r.  What common concerns of my target audience will my book address?

s.  What actions should my readers take to solve their problems?

t.  What actions should my readers cease to solve their problems?

u.  Do I have a system, process, or methodology that could help the reader? If so, consider including that in the book (e.g., *"7 Steps to Overcoming Procrastination"*)

v.  What common myths are there that aren't true or don't work for most?

w.  What common attitudes delay my readers' success?

x.  What attitudes should my readers adopt?

y.  What common beliefs delay my readers' success?

z.  What beliefs should my reader adopt?

aa. What are my readers' correct behaviors that I should applaud?

ab. What common mistakes do people make?

ac. How can they avoid making those mistakes?

ad. What success stories can I share that would help my readers learn what to do?

ae. What inspiration stories can I share that would help my readers learn what to do?

af. What mistake or failure stories can I share that would help my readers learn what not to do?

ag. How can I help my readers learn and grow?

6) Know that not everyone will encourage your writing. Do not let them abort your journey.

7) You will need Persistent Mental Stamina.

8) Decide the length of your book – 10,000 words equal 90 minutes of reading.

9) Decide the book title.

10) Decide the book subtitle.

11) Designate your writing space.

12) Eliminate distractions from your writing space.

13) Collect your writing tools - pen, pencil, and paper.

14) Cursive write. Research proves that cursive writing improves brain development in the areas of thinking, language, and working memory. Cursive handwriting stimulates the brain synapses and synchronicity between the left and right hemispheres, something absent from printing and typing.

15) Pre-sell thirty (30) books.

16) START!

### Module #2 ~ Writing

1) Regularly backup and save your document.

2) Store your document in the cloud and/or at an offsite location.

3) Develop your book's proposition.

4) Begin researching, retrieving, and documenting information.

5) Sketch out the Table of Contents.

6) Outline – chronologically, geographically, spatial, climatic, topical, and psychological.

7) Chronological organization - concerns itself with narration, process, cause and effect. It uses words and phrases like next, later, the following day, and afterwards, to make transitions.

8) Geographical organization – concerns itself with land location or relationship location as in one item's proximity to another.

9) Spatial organization – concerns itself with physical position or relationship. It uses words and phrases like just to the right, a little further on, to the south of, a few feet behind and six inches above, to make transitions.

10) Climatic organization – concerns itself with an order of importance. It uses words and phrases like more importantly, best of all, still worse, and a more effective approach, to make transitions.

11) Topical organization – concerns itself with classification and division, comparison and contrasts, analogy, and definition. It uses words like: the first element, another key part, and a third common principle to make transitions.

12) Psychological organization – concerns itself with the flowchart of comprehension. It uses words and phrases like general to specific, most familiar to least familiar, and simple to complex, to make transitions.

13) Start writing - Do not edit as you go and do not critique. Write every idea that comes to mind. Do not delete anything as you go. Do not concern yourself with errors.

14) When you write, let yourself escape into the open and land on paper.

15) Find your niche and write what you know.

16) Brand yourself and your ideas.

17) Make substantiated definitive statements.

18) Create a memorable presentation by writing for your target audience.

19) Place each major section in the outline or idea on a separate page. When you write, write under the section where materials fit.

20) Regularly write a minimum number of words, for a period or exhaust a thought block.

21) Solicit early and regular feedback. After 2,500; 5,000 and 10,000 words, I will peruse and give feedback.

22) Find objective readers – Beware the praises or critiques of your great aunt Edna. In most cases, you'd be better off joining a local writers' group. The authors in these groups can provide tremendous feedback, inspire new ideas, and give great moral support. Writing is often a very solitary pursuit, and these groups can be your "lifeline." Digest their commentary; be surprised at their insights and your blind spots; dust yourself off and revise if necessary.

23) Do include personal examples.

24) Write in active voice.

25) Avoid clichés.

26) Focus on the Verbs.

27) Keep verbs near to the subject.

28) Use alliteration - the occurrence of the same letter or sound at the beginning of adjacent or closely connected words. "Love the life you live. Live the life you love." Bob Marley

29) Make your writing engaging and exciting.

30) Anticipate questions and answer them in advance. Your reader will not have the luxury of asking you questions.

31) Be specific.

32) Make every word count.

33) Vividly detail and describe everything.

34) Include both genders.

35) Invoke multiple senses. For example, "Just as I began to smell the roses, I saw the snake lying in the bushes." "Just as I felt the chilly wind tingling my arms, I heard the car door slam."

36) Evoke strong emotions. "Storming into the house, I angrily confronted the teenager for throwing the rock."

37) Create interesting characters.

38) Pull the reader into the action.

39) Overcome objections lodged in the mind of your audience.

40) Make the reader believe you.

41) Include a call to action.

42) Write a series of summaries, 800-1200 words about your book, but in different perspectives or viewpoints. These summaries may help reveal what's most essential about your book. Reading them should help clarify the core essentials of your story, the relative strength of your characters or topics, and perhaps even provide clues about how to best structure your book.

43) Read your book out loud.

44) Your book is finished when everybody is reasonably happy. The decision to say, "It's really the end" will always be yours alone.

45) Presell another thirty (30) more books.

46) START.

47) KEEP WRITING.

## Module #3 ~ Rewriting

1) Add some more words but avoid unnecessary padding.

2) Remove some words.

3) Replace some words.

4) Rearrange some words.

5) Focus on the verbs.

6) Remove as many adjectives as possible.

7) Search for more powerful alternate adjectives.

8) Search for more powerful alternate adverbs.

9) Pay close attention to:

    a. Phrases

    b. Sentences

    c. Sentence structure

    d. Paragraphs

    e. Pages

    f. Chapters

    g. Sections

10) <u>Conceptual editing</u> strives to bring about clear ideology and ease of understanding. To achieve this goal, different types of writing organization must be considered.

11) <u>Grammatical editing</u> strives to correct:

    a. Words and sentences, making them clearer, more precise, and thus, more effective.

b. Spelling

   c. Capitalization

   d. Punctuation

   e. Run-on sentences

   f. Verb tenses

   g. Wordiness

   h. Plurals

   i. Possessives

   j. Pronoun antecedent agreement

   k. Modifiers

   l. Subject verb agreements.

12) <u>Contextual editing</u> strives to bring about correct coherence between sections of the writing. Answering these questions will help:

   a. Does this sentence contribute to this writing? How?

   b. Does this sentence contribute to this paragraph? How?

   c. Does this paragraph contribute to this writing? How?

   d. Does this paragraph contribute to this section? How?

   e. Does this section contribute to this writing? How?

   f. Does this section best contribute in its present location? How?

13) Employ a professional editor. People are accustomed to reading books that have been polished by the editing process. The editing process prunes the writing, making good writing even better. Through editing, the book is refined from an amateurish to a professional piece of prose. Editing does not strip your personality from the writing. Yet, it will make the true nature of your writing shine forth by removing superfluous fluff and re-crafting the textual

tone of the writing. Professional editing is an absolute must if you want your book to reach its full potential. Even the most polished writer can benefit from editing. Professional editing brings another set of eyes to do a final read-through checking spelling and punctuation.

    a. Proofreading – the simplest and most affordable form of editing, proofreading is for writers who don't need help with the contents of the book itself, but who need someone to simply go over the text for basic grammatical and spelling errors.

    b. Line Editing – line editing will determine if your manuscript has plot holes, limited characterization, factual errors, and/or syntactical problems. Line editing— (tightens wordiness, turns passive voice "active," plus corrects spelling/grammar/punctuation/style).

14) Presell another thirty (30) books.

15) Start thinking about writing your next book.

I have performed some part in coaching and/or publishing for:

| | |
|---|---|
| Williams, Steve | The Master's Call |
| Harris, Loyd | The Hour Has Come |
| White, I. V. | This Is My Story |
| Leonard, Minnie | This Old House (Poems) |
| Leonard, Minnie | Poetry Inspired From God's Word |
| Cleveland, Aretha | Talking Faith Walking Fear |
| Cleveland, Aretha | My Foundation Is Cracking I Need A New Contractor |
| Cleveland, Aretha | Be Free |
| Ray, Monica | Learning To Splash – Conquering the Life You Have Been Given |
| Reg'ena, Karen | In My Mother's Voice |
| Watson, Candace | Ice: Careful Don't Burn Yourself |

## Module #4 ~ Post Writing

1) Determine a title and a subtitle. One strikes the intellect; the other ignites the emotions.

2) Decide who will write your foreword, preface, and/or introduction.

   a. Foreword – spelled just like that and not 'forward' or 'foreward'– is a short piece of writing found at the start of the book or piece of literature and written by someone other than the primary author of the literature. The foreword basically talks about the interaction or relationship between the author of the book and the author of the foreword. It can also be an expert in the field that talks about the theories covered in the book or the paper. It can also include respect from a well-acclaimed author of today. The easiest way to remember is that the foreword is usually written by another author that may be a more established author in the same field or someone who wishes to pay respect to the author that has written the article. Foreword is also often used as a marketing technique by publishers that promote a new book and author by having a famous person write positive things about the book.

   b. A preface is a short piece of literature that is written by the author of the book or paper himself. The preface usually follows the foreword, if it also presents the literature. The preface generally tells how the story of the book came into being; how the idea of the story came to the author and any other interesting tidbits that the author can come up with to keep the reader interested. The preface usually ends with thanks and acknowledgments to people who were helpful to the author during the time of writing. A preface is usually signed, followed by the date and place of writing.

   c. An introduction is a piece of literature that is written by the author and found in books, essays, or article. The information is more commonly a part of essays and papers, rather than books. It is the beginning section of a literature that states the purpose and goals of the writing the literature. The introduction gives a sneak peek into what the reader should expect to read in the rest of the paper or the book. Information essential to the main text is generally placed in a set of explanatory notes, which may be paginated with Arabic numerals. In technical writing, the preface and foreword can be a part of the introduction, but it can also stand apart.

3) Share sections of your book with your peers and gather back cover page testimonials for your book.

4) Decide mood and style of cover.

5) Visit Barnes & Noble or another major bookstore. Examine books that you like. Note the color, font style, font size, design, shapes, titles, photos, and subtitles. Select the ones that you would like to utilize for your book and share with your graphics designer.

6) Design book cover: The main goal of every book cover is to generate excitement and attract attention. Millions of potential readers will only know your work by a quick glance at your cover. A brilliant cover is the absolute best tool in your future marketing arsenal. It's your anchor point for all your promotions, a graphical symbol of your book. *Your cover should engage readers in such a way that they're inspired to buy your book.* Your front cover is the image of your book that you have chosen to put out to the world. Invariably, the book cover design is also the most significant piece of marketing that a book can have. It should look as good as a traditionally published book. The graphic artist will assist with selecting color, images, font size, style, color, and design for both the front and back cover.

7) Employ a graphic design artist. Your book must be typeset. From your manuscript, the typesetter will illustrate the materials and set them on a page ready for printing. Consider books whose author received a huge cash advance. Those publishers have conducted much research. Study their productions.

a. <u>Inside text</u>
The graphic artist will select the font style and size, line leading, hyphenation settings, margins, spacing between words, and lines, paragraph alignment, and page layout. The layout will reflect the subject and style of writing. Also, the graphic artist will lay out the sections, and align chapter title pages, and page numbering.

b. <u>Outside book cover</u>
*Your cover should engage readers in such a way that they're inspired to buy your book.* Your front cover is the image of your book that you have chosen to put out to the world. Invariably, the book cover design is also the most significant piece of marketing that a book can have. It should look as good as a traditionally published book. The graphic artist will assist with selecting color, images, font size, style, color, and design for both the front and back cover.

8) Some of your close friends will never buy your book.

9) Some of your close friends will ask for a discount. Decide now not to give discounts.

10) Pre-sell another 30 books.

11) Prepare and schedule a Press Release.

12) By releasing your book at a major event, you can jumpstart sales.

13) Ask speakers at seminars, who will be speaking on subject matter addressed in your book, to recommend and sell your book at their sessions.

14) Share your book with book clubs.

15) Join a local writers guild.

16) Join or start a book reading club.

17) Release your book on Amazon.com. Become active in *Goodreads,* an Amazon community of readers.

18) Create a virtual tour of your book.

19) Reach out to your high school classmates and university alumni.

20) Place an office copy of your book in waiting rooms (e.g., offices of attorneys, dentists, doctors, auto service departments, etc).

21) Become a member of the John Marshall Publishing conglomerate.

22) Write another book and advertise each book in each book.

23) Sell your book – Daily.

    a. Place a post on Facebook.
    b. Place a post on Twitter.
    c. Place a post on LinkedIn.
    d. Instagram
    e. Pinterest
    f. Distribute business cards that advertise your book.
    g. Always keep copies of your book and sell them from your inventory rather than send customers to Amazon. Your profit is higher when you eliminate the middleman.

24) Sell your book – Weekly.
    a. Give a discount for sales at a fundraiser.
    b. Schedule book signings
    c. Place books on consignment at different businesses
    d. Email an excerpt of the book and/or a virtual tour of the book to your database
    e. Blog

25) Sell your book – Monthly.
    a. Speak at events and sell your book.
    b. Create a workshop based on a topic of your book.
    c. Set up vendor booths at events and sell your book.
    d. Partner with speakers. Ask them to recommend your book when they are speaking on topics your book addresses.

26) Paraphernalia

    a. Ask me about my book (title) T-shirts.

    b. Ask me about my spouse, parent, mother, and friend's book T-shirts.

    c. Ask me about my book ink pens.

    d. Ask me about my book drinking container.

    e. Ask me about my book iPad cover.

    f. Create an E-Book

27) Promote! Promote! Promote!

28) To obtain ISBN #  https://www.isbn-us.com/home1/

29) Printing Companies

    a. https://myaccount.ingramspark.com
    b. https://www.docucopies.com/

I am not promising you that I can make you a nationally known author who floods the New York Times best-seller list, but I guarantee that I can coach you to the phases that will produce a quality book.

# PUBLISHING

**PARENTING**
One good place to deposit wisdom is into your posterity. If you are up to the parenting challenge, do it. But unfortunately, there is a major problem. The juvenile-lization of America had made parenting more difficult. Adverse juvenile-lization is the process by which adolescents' beliefs, practices, and developmental characteristics become accepted as appropriate *by* adults. Through this, parents sink into a position to satisfy the demands of their children. Removing all suppression and giving your children an opportunity to express their thoughts and feelings can grow a healthy self-concept within your children. However, the parents must reserve the total right to veto and overrule the children's preferences if need be. And they must exercise that right without any negative responses from the children.

Reverse juvenile-lization is the process by which the beliefs, practices and developmental characteristics of adolescents become accepted as appropriate *for* adults. Through this, parents sink into position to imitate the behavior of children. Allowing parents to express themselves youthfully can grow healthy self-concept within adults. However, parents must distinguish themselves from their children. At times, parents may need to forgo their preference to further establish the identity of their role as a parent.

What would you like to change between you and your children? In other words, what is the problem? You must discover the problem before you pursue the solution. Work to better recognize the problem so that you can determine the best solution.

**Parenting is a Heart Job!**
God designed the universe as a system and as systems within a system. A system consists of patterns, principles, and procedures. Patterns, principles, and procedures are just established ways of doing things.

In addition to the system of the visible material universe, God also designed the system of the invisible immaterial universe. Within the invisible immaterial universe, He placed patterns, principles, and procedures. He placed the patterns, principles, and procedures within the invisible immaterial universe to guide and guard the material universe: gravity, condensation, evaporation, etc. (Amos 5:8; 9:6, Isaiah 55:8-10, Jeremiah 10:12-13; 51:16).

God organizes and administers the universe by system. Family organization and administration are done by system. Every problem can be successfully managed through system design. Yes, organize and administer your family by system. For effective family organization and administration through a system you must:

Discover the present system [patterns, principles, and procedures] within your family. Which are progressive - leads the family healthily forward? Which are regressive – leads the family unhealthily backward? Now you have a clearer view of the problem.

Design out the problem. For example, if your son keeps turning the television on in the morning, being late, and missing the bus, disconnect the television and remove it from his room.


Design in the solution. Write a set of definitive steps that he must follow each day to prepare for school.

Design out the impediment. Remove all other distractions. Require him to take all his clothes, go into the bathroom, and dress there for school. There are fewer distractions in the bathroom.

Design in progress. Reward your children's positive behavior. Do not just punish their negative behavior. Negotiate their rewards.


**Discipline**
Discipline is the process by which parents make disciples of their children. Establish reasonable expectations, set, and enforce limits. Parents must model socially appropriate behavior.

Implement discipline; not to make your children happy but do make them behave in a civilized manner. Keep the family family-centered (marriage and/or adult-centered). Do not allow the family to become child centered. I repeat, do not become a child-centered parent. The child fits into the family. The family does not adapt to fit the child.
Parents must command respect by being an authoritative model who demands proper moral conduct from children. You are an agent of the community, not just an advocate for your child.

Every child needs to accept responsibility by doing uncompensated chores within the household. The child does chores because, and only because, he/she is a member of the family.

Always supervise occasional involvement. Allow your child to be liberated, but within limits. Create distinct boundaries. There should be times when your child is seen and not heard.


Military and jail
Rule # 1:
From this point on, you will pay much more attention to me than I will ever again give to you.

Rule # 2:
You will do as I say.

Rule # 3:
You will do what I say, not because of bribery, brutality, or persuasive explanation. You will do as I say because I say so. Period! Give them reasons but tell them that they must do what you say. Do not entertain the idea of allowing them to renege.


## **Monitor**

I) Visit your child's school during the first week of school.

II) Actively participate in the parent/teacher organization.

III) Randomly visit and sit in class.

IV) Provide academically challenging resources for children – beyond what the school provides.

V) Never punish by withholding academics, but rather by adding.

VI) Know whose environment your child is in 24/7.

VII) Parent your children's friends closely.

VIII) Monitor the 20 minutes before the child leaves home and the first 20 upon return. This reinforces the "there is always an adult in control" notion, but it also allows parents to welcome their child from the day's brutal events.

IX) Celebrate milestones.

X) Teach your children their cultural history against the backdrop of your family (Deuteronomy 5-6).

XI) Nurture their natural curiosity.

XII) Occasionally, disconnect the television, telephone, and other electronic stimulators.

XIII) Monitor their diet.

XIV) Develop a system to solve every life issue.

XV) Train children to prepare everything the night before for the next day.

XVI) Occasionally, snoop.

# PEER PRESSURE

Pilate discovered that Jesus was innocent (John 18:38, 19:4, 6). So why did he release Him to be crucified (John 19:16)? Pilate surrendered to the peer pressure from the Jews (John 19:12-13).

Our peers are those from whom we seek the favor of approval Psychologists label them our "significant others". Influence from our "significant others" is called peer pressure. Peer pressure influences young and old, as well as sinner and saint. The influence of peer pressure may be constructive (Hebrews 10:23-24), it may also be destructive (Acts 5:9). You can successfully resist the influence of destructive peer pressure.

### Investigate the Nickels

Nickels (money) are avenues through which our peers influence us. With nickels, the Jews influenced Pilate (John 19:12-13; 16; Luke 23:1-2). Caesar received the tax money and allocated Pilate's financial resources. Therefore, the Jews attacked Pilate's allegiance to Caesar. Nickels destroyed Pilate's better judgment. He then surrendered to the peer pressure (John 19:12-13; 16). Investigate the nickels by asking:

1) Is my integrity for sale?
2) May I earn sufficiently without selling my integrity? 3) Where will this trend eventually lead me?

Remember that unethical and unfair gain is shortly lived and shallowly enjoyed.

### Ignore the Noise

Noise is an avenue through which our peers influence us. With noise, the Jews influenced Pilate (Matthew 27:21-26). Pilate attempted to stop a riot by releasing a murderous rioter (Mark 15:7; Luke 23:18-25). Noise destroyed Pilate's better judgment. He then surrendered to the peer pressure. Ignore the noise by asking:

1) What are these people really saying?

2) Are they arguing wisely or foolishly?

Remember that you can say no and not feel guilty.

**Interpret the Numbers**

Numbers are avenues through which our peers influence us. With the numbers, the Jews influenced Pilate (Matthew 27:20). Only a woman, Pilate's wife, spoke on behalf of Jesus (Matthew 27:19). He attempted to solve the problem by consenting with the majority. The numbers destroyed Pilate's better judgment. He then surrendered to the peer pressure. Interpret the numbers by asking:

1) Who are these people who say this? 2) Are they losers who desire company?

Remember that the Lord does not have the majority on His side. He has had the majority on His side only twice during human history: immediately after the creation and after the flood.

**The First Most Important Exercise of Wisdom**

Eventually, each one of us will transition into eternity in one of two places: heaven or hell. Those in heaven will spend eternity in the presence of God. Those not in heaven will spend eternity away from the presence of God. The decision you make while alive on earth will dictate where you spend eternity. This decision about eternity is the most important decision.

## BECOME SAVED
### The Basis of Salvation

The first mention of blood was Abel's (Genesis 4:10). The last mention of blood was Jesus' (Revelation 19:13). In between times, God sprinkled blood around, about, and all upon His people (Exodus 24:6-8, 29:15-21).

Scripture reveals that the blood of Christ cleanses us from the guilt of sin as we are born into the family of God (1 Peter 1:17-19; Revelation 1:4-6). Grace made the cleansing power of the blood available, but faith activates it (Exodus 12-14; 1 Corinthians 10:1-4).

Scripture reveals that the blood of Christ cleanses us from the guilt of sin after we are born into the family of God (1 John 1:5-2:1; Ephesians 1:3-8). Forgiveness is durative even for those who are not living a perfectly sinless life.

God wants you to think thoroughly about the blood of Jesus. Never ask, "Can God forgive the sinner?" On the basis of the blood of Jesus, God can forgive sinners. Never ask, "Will God forgive the saint?" On the basis of the blood of Jesus, God will forgive saints. God wants you to celebrate the power of the blood (Exodus 12:13, 1 Corinthians 10:1-4; John 19:34). God is a bloody God. The bible is a bloody book. Believers, God's people, are a bloody people.

Moses negotiated with Pharaoh for the release of the Israelites from captivity. Only after the Passover, the tenth plague, did Pharaoh release the Israelites. But, as they traveled toward the Promised Land, Pharaoh changed his mind and pursued after them.

With his army, Pharaoh sandwiched the Israelites against the Red Sea (Exodus 14:5-9). God provided salvation (Exodus 14:13-14). Salvation was a military term describing an escape from a position of danger to a position of safety.

Salvation is a deliverance from an old relationship. In their old relationship, they served Pharaoh (Exodus 1:8-14; 5:1-14). In our old relationship, we served sin (John 8:34, Romans 6:16-17). Actively, we do that which the Lord does not authorize (1 John 3:4). Passively, we refuse to do that which the Lord does authorize (James 4:17; Luke 12:47-48).

Salvation is a deliverance from an old relationship to a new relationship. In their new relationship, they served Moses. In our new relationship, we serve righteousness (Romans 6:16-18). Actively, we do that which the Lord authorizes. Passively, we refuse to do that which the Lord does not authorize.

Of the several types of salvation the Bible speaks of, the relationships delivered from and to may differ; however, the principle of the process of the deliverance remains the same. Salvation takes place according to an authorized process.

A) For their salvation from Pharaoh:
 1) The Lord, who provided salvation, responded.
 2) The Lord's spokesperson, who informed them of the salvation, responded.
 3) The endangered people, who needed to receive the salvation, responded.

God provided this salvation for them and Paul called it a baptism (1 Corinthians 10:1-2). This process was: (a) necessary, (b) different, (c) humanly illogical, but (d) successful.

B) For our salvation from sin:
 1) The Lord, who provides salvation, has responded. He sent Jesus as your sin substitute.
 2) The Lord's spokesperson, informs you of salvation.
 3) The endangered people, you, who need to receive this salvation, need to respond.

Salvation from sin is a deliverance from an old relationship to a new relationship by way of an authorized process. This process was: (a) necessary, (b) different, (c) humanly illogical, but (d) successful. Salvation is not a biological, economical, or racial issue, but a scriptural issue (2 Timothy 3:15). The blood was shed (Exodus 12:1-28). Yet, Israel had not been freed from their slavery to Egypt. Why? There was something they needed to do. They had to go through the waters of baptism (Exodus 14:21-25, 1 Corinthians 10:1-2).

The blood of Jesus has been made available. Unfortunately, all are not saved. Why? Reconciliation was accomplished at the cross but is appropriated at conversion (baptism). Those who are unsaved have not come to enjoy the appropriation of the blood of Jesus. For example: The college student's school loan for the year is accomplished when the university approves it, but the loan is appropriated at the beginning of each semester when the student registers. Your earnings are accomplished each hour, but appropriated when you receive the paycheck.

Many are unsaved because they have no faith response to the resurrection of Jesus. Salvation is accomplished for them, but not yet appropriated to them. Salvation will be appropriated to them when they engage in the behavior (baptism) that leads to salvation.

**First Implementation of God's Plan of Salvation (Acts 2)**

The law of "first mention" may be said to be the principle that requires you to go to that portion of the Scripture where a doctrine is mentioned for the first time and to study the first occurrence of the same in order to get the fundamental inherent meaning of that doctrine. When you thus see the first appearance, which is usually in the simplest form, you can then examine the doctrine in other portions of the Word that were given later. You shall see that the fundamental concept in the first occurrence remains dominant as a rule and directs (interprets) all later additions to that doctrine.

**HEAR THE GOSPEL -** In order for you to be saved, you must hear the gospel. The gospel is the good news of the availability of the salvation that has been provided for by the grace of God and the sacrificial blood of Jesus. The death, burial, and the resurrection of Jesus are the certified facts of the gospel (1 Corinthians 15:1-4). Hearing the gospel is one of the certified obedience requirements of the gospel.

Acts 2:1-4: The apostles preached a Holy Spirit-directed sermon. This was the first sermon preached to unsaved people after the resurrection of Jesus. Therefore, we can apply the "law of first mention".

Acts 2:6-8: In their own (native) language, the people heard the Holy Spirit-directed sermon.

Acts 2:29-33: The people heard the certified facts (death, burial, resurrection) of the gospel of Jesus Christ.
Acts 2:36-37: Hearing the fact of the resurrection of Jesus, the Man they had crucified, pierced their heart. Yes, this sermon irritated their conscience.

**BELIEVE THE GOSPEL** - In order for you to be saved, you must believe the gospel. To believe the gospel is to intellectually and emotionally embrace the facts of the death, burial, and resurrection of Jesus.

Acts 2:12-16: Though they understood verbally what was said, at first some did not know the meaning of the message experience. Therefore, they asked, *"...What does this mean?"* Some of the people suggested that the apostles were experiencing drunkenness. Therefore, they said, *"...They are full of sweet wine."*

Acts 2:22-24: Though they did not initially know the meaning of this message, when they were reminded of the ministry of Jesus, they could not help but believe their knowledge of what God had done through Jesus.

Acts 2:32-33: God had raised Jesus from the dead and exalted Him. Again, they were reminded of what they had already observed *"..we are all witnesses. ... this which you both see and hear."*

Acts 2:37: Because they believed that God had raised up to life the very Man they had put down to death, the preached word pierced their heart, and irritated their conscience.
Acts 2:41: Because they had come to believe that Jesus was the Son of God, they received the word.

**REPENT OF SIN** - In order for you to be saved, you must repent. Repentance is your change of heart that takes place in your mind (Matthew 21:28-32). In repentance, you change your allegiance (Acts 17:30, 26:19-20). Repentance is a resetting of your allegiance. It is a resetting of your allegiance from your selfish self to the Savior.

Acts 2:38: The Holy Spirit led the apostle Peter to command the people to repent of having opposed God, *"Peter said to them, repent..."*
Acts 2:41-42: Earlier, they rejected the word and crucified Jesus. But now,

they are receiving the word and embracing Jesus as the Son of God. This change of heart indicates their repentance.

**CONFESS THAT JESUS IS THE SON OF GOD** - In order for you to be saved, you must confess. What does it mean to confess? Confess is translated from a compound word (homlogeo) that means to speak the same. Therefore, to confess is to admit (John 1:20, 12:42). To confess is to acknowledge (Romans 10:9, 14:10-12, Hebrews 13:15). Confess means that you agree at heart and speak the same thing as another (1 John 1:10).

Acts 2:37: God said that Jesus is His Son (Matthew 3:16-17). Therefore, the people must admit that Jesus was the Son of God. By asking, *"what shall we do"*, they admitted that they had come to believe the gospel that had been preached. Yes, they agreed with and acknowledged the truth of the fact that Jesus was the Son of God.

**BECOME BAPTIZED** – In order for you to be saved, you must be baptized. Baptism is your faith response of being buried in water in response to the fact that Jesus Christ is the Son of God (Acts 8:12; 37-39; 1 Peter 3:21). Baptism is mentioned some 92 times in the New Testament. Interestingly, Jesus began His earthly ministry being baptized of John in the Jordan River (Matthew 3:13-17) and concluded His ministry by commanding His apostles to baptize those who would become His disciples (Matthew 28:19-20). **Obviously, baptism is essential.**

Acts 2:38: The Holy Spirit led the apostle Peter to command them to *"... be baptized in the name of Jesus Christ for the forgiveness of our sins..."* The purpose for which they were to become baptized harmonized with the earlier statement of Jesus (Mark 16:16). This was the first time the apostles had ever taught about baptism. This was the first time the apostles had ever told a person to become baptized. Though Jesus had taught the relationship between baptism and salvation, this was the first time the apostles had ever taught the inherent relationship between baptism and salvation. The "law of first mention" must be considered in this instance.

Acts 2:40-42: Obviously, those in the audience believed that there existed an inherent relationship between baptism and salvation, for 3,000 people who received His word were baptized that same day.

# BECOME SAVED
## The Relationship Between Baptism and Salvation

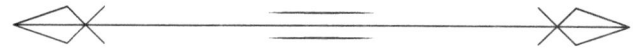

*Read: Mark 16:16*
Where did Jesus place baptism; before salvation or after salvation?

Why is there so much confusion on the subject of baptism? An intellectual "exegesis" [reading out of] of scripture rather than an emotional "eisegesis" [reading into] of scripture peels away most of the layers of confusion. Let's proceed.

The Holy Spirit could not come until after Jesus had risen from the dead and ascended to heaven (John 16:7). Some 40 days after Jesus had risen from the dead, the Holy Spirit was yet to come (Acts 1:1-8). The Holy Spirit came on the day of Pentecost (Acts 2:1-4).

The Holy Spirit revealed the message of truth to those who wrote scripture (Ephesians 3:1-5, 2 Peter 1:21). The apostle Peter spoke the words of Acts 2:38 before Matthew, Mark, Luke, and John wrote the words contained in their Gospels. Being from regions beyond Jerusalem, most of those who heard the words of Acts 2:38 had not heard Jesus speak (Acts 2:9-11). Even those who had heard Jesus speak had failed to understand His message; therefore, they crucified Him (John 20:30, Acts 3:29).

Historically, the Jews had offered sacrifices with an understanding that they would invoke the forgiveness (appeasement) of God. Even on Pentecost, they believed that they needed to respond in order to receive forgiveness of God. Therefore, they asked, "What shall we do" (Acts 2:37).

Peter had just preached a persuasive sermon designed to convince the audience that Jesus was the Christ and Lord (Acts 2:36). Obviously, some who heard, also believed, for their hearts were pricked (Acts 2:37). Hearts are never pricked until belief comes. In addition to believing, they asked what to do. In other words, they were now asking, "After believing what (else) shall we do? If they had been forgiven [saved] just by believing, then Peter should have told them so. Otherwise, he accommodated their false belief about doing something, in addition to believing in order to be saved.

In the past, they had killed and offered an animal in their effort to receive forgiveness of sins. Peter informed them that no longer would they have to kill a lamb. The Lamb (Jesus) had already been slain. They must now repent and be baptized to embrace the death of Jesus.
Only after Jesus had been raised from the dead did He teach of the cause and effect relationship of baptism with salvation.

But what about Romans 10:9-10? Let's set the stage.

1. Those to whom the apostle Paul addressed this letter were called and had become saints (see Romans 1:6-7).

2. They had died to sin (see Romans 6:2).

3. They had been baptized into Christ and His death (see Romans 6:3).

4. They had been raised from the dead to walk in the newness of life (see Romans 6:4).

5. They had become united with Jesus (see Romans 6:5).

6. Their old self had been crucified with Christ (see Romans 6:6).

7. They had obeyed from the heart the doctrinal teachings (see Romans 6:17).

8. They had been freed from sin (see Romans 6:18).

9. They had become servants of righteousness (see Romans 6:18).

Believers from Rome had been at Pentecost and likely had been baptized then (Acts 2:10). Hence, the apostle Paul said to the believers, those who had already been baptized "confess and believe" (Romans 10:9-10).

Many people have read or heard this, *"for by grace you have been saved through faith"* and concluded that grace and faith excludes baptism (Ephesians 2:8). It is true that the apostle wrote this statement about the believers of Ephesus. What can we definitely know from scripture that will shed light on the subject? Let's look further.

Had not the Ephesians, those in Ephesus, heard the message of truth (Ephesians 1:13)? Had not the Ephesians, those in Ephesus, believed the message of truth?

Had not the Ephesians, those in Ephesus, been baptized? Acts 19:1-5

Those believers to whom the apostle Paul wrote, had heard the gospel, believed the gospel, and had been baptized. The grace and faith that saved them included baptism.

## BECOME SAVED
### Holy Spirit-led Post Resurrection Understanding of Baptism

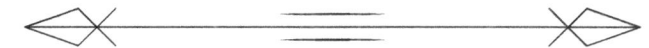

Most of the biblical information about baptism comes after Jesus had been resurrected from the dead. The Holy Spirit guided the apostles and prophets as they spoke and wrote about baptism. Through the Holy Spirit, God provided a more comprehensive understanding of the role and relationship of baptism.

### Read: Acts 8:26-40
The eunuch did not understand what he was reading from Isaiah 53:7ff (Acts 8:30-32). Philip began at Isaiah 53:7, the place where the eunuch was reading, and preached unto him Jesus (Acts 8:35).

How could Philip preach Jesus when the name Jesus is not once stated in Isaiah 53?

How could Philip demand that the eunuch believe that Jesus Christ is the Son of God when believing that Jesus Christ is the Son of God is never stated in Isaiah 53?

How could Philip introduce the subject of baptism while preaching Jesus from Isaiah 53 when baptism is not stated in Isaiah 53?

How could Philip understand Isaiah 53 when the eunuch did not?

The answers to all four questions are the same. Philip had a Holy Spirit-led post-resurrection understanding of the Old Testament scripture (Acts 6:5) and the eunuch did not.

God had more fully revealed His will to the apostles and prophets (Ephesians 3:5). There are some things that had not been understood before, but came to be understood only after the resurrection of Jesus and the coming enlightening provided through the Holy Spirit. Because Philip had a Holy Spirit-led post-resurrection understanding of the Old Testament scripture, God enlightened him to understand things more fully than did others. God enlightened His apostles and prophets to understand the Old Testament. When we read the New Testament, we gain insight into the inspired minds of the apostles and prophets (Ephesians 3:5).

Jesus recognized that men needed a post-resurrection understanding of the Old Testament scripture. Therefore, He opened their minds to understand the scriptures (Luke 24:44-47).

God opened Lydia's mind to understand (Acts 16:14). Her understanding led to her being baptized (Acts 16:15).

Where does Old Testament teach the purpose of baptism? It does not; it just illustrates it. The lamb's blood became available for the Israelites (Exodus 12:21-28). Yet, the Israelites were not free from bondage until they passed through the sea (Exodus 14:26-29). God saved Israel on the day that they passed through the water (Exodus 14:30). The Holy Spirit's inspired commentary called that experience a baptism, *"For I do not want you to be unaware, brethren, that our fathers were all under the cloud and all passed through the sea; and all were baptized into Moses in the cloud and in the* sea; and all ate the same spiritual food; and all drank the same spiritual drink, for they were drinking from a spiritual rock which followed them; and the rock was Christ" (1 Corinthians 10:1-4).

# BECOME SAVED
## The Dry Side of Baptism

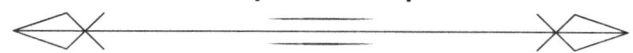

**Read: Matthew 28:18-20**
When did Jesus teach about baptism, before or after salvation?

**Read: Mark 16:15-18**
What did Jesus say were the prerequisites of salvation?

**Read: Acts 2:38**
What did the apostle Peter say was the purpose of baptism?

To His apostles, Jesus made a few final remarks after His resurrection. Baptism was one of the topics that He discussed with them (Matthew 28:18-20; Mark 16:15-18). Clearly, the baptism of new believers is of vital significance to the Lord Jesus. God-fearing believers want to know that Christ approves of their baptism. Our baptism indicates that the reality of our death with Christ is a realized fact. Our baptism indicates that the reality of our death with Christ is a ruling force. Near the beginning of his ministry, the apostle Peter preached about baptism (Acts 2:38). Near the ending of his ministry, the apostle Peter wrote about baptism.

**Read: 1 Peter 3:21**
What does this text say that baptism does?

Indeed, the apostle Peter reminded the believers of the importance of baptism. First, we consider the "dry" side of baptism. It is a response of the mind; for it is an internal appeal toward God. The dry side is a response of the *conscience.* The conscience is a product of accepted teachings (John 8:1-9; Leviticus 20:10). If you have been taught to be honest and you accept that as valid, whenever you are dishonest you violate your conscience. Your conscience then causes you to feel guilty. On the other hand, if you were taught to be honest and you consider that invalid, then you do not violate your conscience. Therefore, you feel no guilt.

The dry side is a response of a ***good conscience.*** Within this context, a good conscience is a heart that trusts in the resurrection of Jesus Christ (1 Peter 3: 21). The resurrection proves that Jesus is the Son of God (Romans 1:4; Acts 17:31). Only those who believe in the resurrection of Jesus have a good conscience for baptism (John 8:24; Acts 8:35-37).

If one's conscience is insufficiently taught, then it will be insufficiently developed. And if one's conscience is incorrectly taught, then it will be incorrectly developed. A good conscience results from having accepted wholesome teachings. When taught insufficiently, conscience insufficiently develops (Acts 19:1-5). When taught erroneously, then conscience erroneously develops.

The Israelites, after seeing the power of God displayed through him, were baptized into Moses as their deliverer (Exodus 14:31; 1 Corinthians 10:2). We, after hearing about the power of God displayed through the resurrection of Jesus, (Romans 1:1-4) are then baptized into Christ as our Savior. To identify with Jesus and rely on Him for salvation from sin, we must be baptized.

### What really happens at baptism?
John the Baptist announced that he baptized in water, but that Jesus would baptize with the Holy Spirit (Matthew 3:11; Mark. 1:8; Luke. 3:16; John 1:33). He made this statement to the general population before Jesus ever began choosing His apostles. What did he mean?

By the Holy Spirit, Jesus baptizes us all into the one body of Christ (1 Corinthians 12:13). Persons whom Jesus baptizes by the Holy Spirit are all truly members of His one body, without regard to earthly distinctions (1 Corinthians 12:13; Galatians 3:2627; Ephesians 2:18). The baptism work of the Holy Spirit has to do with the body of Christ, the church. By the Spirit baptism we are immersed into the body of Christ. Here, the Spirit is the instrument, the agent who places the believer into the body of Christ. The creation of the one body is the result of the baptism work of the Holy Spirit. At the moment of salvation, the baptism work of the Holy Spirit inducts the believer as a living member into the body of Christ.

They, who are baptized by the Holy Spirit, may continue to draw refreshment and spiritual nourishment from that same inexhaustible source (John 4:1314; John 7:3739). Speaking in tongues is not the indispensable sign of the baptism work of the Holy Spirit. In the first century, even as now, every Christian experienced the baptism work of the Holy Spirit. Not even then in the first century did every Christian speak in tongues (1 Corinthians 12:30).

## BECOME SAVED
### The Wet Side of Baptism

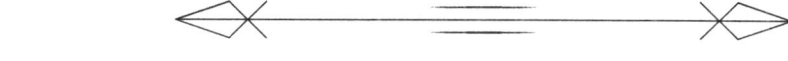

Secondly, we consider the "wet" side of baptism. The wet side is a response of the body; for it is an external appeal towards God. The wet side consists of a **burial in water.**

The word "covenant" is of Latin origin. It is derived from the two words "com" = together and "venire" = to come. It meant a literal coming together.

The corresponding Hebrew word for covenant meant "to cut, to eat" as in the cutting asunder of the victims which were sacrificed at the making of a covenant (Genesis 15:9-21; Jeremiah 34:18-19). To eat, probably referred to the eating of the slain victims. To eat with someone was commonly regarded as almost equivalent to making a covenant with that person (Genesis 31:43-55; Exodus 24:1-2, 9-11).

Offering sacrifices also ratified covenants (Genesis 15:7-21; Exodus 24:3-8; Jeremiah 34:17-22). It was accepted that the sacrificial blood has the sacramental power to bind together two parties in a covenant (1 Corinthians 11:25). The Greeks had two words that conveyed the concept of covenant:

(1) *suntheke* - devoted solemn agreement made between equals
(2) *diatheke* - agreement made by superior for the acceptance and observing of an inferior

All of God's covenants are *diatheke*. A covenant must include three items: (1) covenantor, (2) covenantee, and (3) various stipulations of the contract. A covenant was a firm confirmed commitment (Hebrews 6:13-17).

Through Abram, God teaches us that commitment comes by covenant. Within each covenant there exists the core essence of the covenant and a ceremonial expression of the covenant.

God promised Abram that He would bless all the earth through him and his descendants (Genesis 12:3-5). God revealed the core essence of His covenant with Abram (Genesis 17:16; 19). He then required Abram to participate in the ceremonial expression of His covenant. Participation in the ceremonial expression of the covenant is essential to the strengthening of faith in the core essence of the covenant.

***How would God have responded to Abraham if he neglected to participate in the ceremony of the covenant?***

There is the ceremonial expression (ceremony) of the name change (Genesis 17:3-8; 15). God required Abram to change his and Sarai's name. There is the ceremonial expression of circumcision (Genesis 17:10-14; 23-27). God required Abraham to circumcise himself, his son and his male servants. Participation in the ceremonial expression of the covenant is essential to strengthening faith in the core essence of the covenant. Therefore, the core of the covenant is inherently attached to the ceremonial expression of the covenant. Abraham had to participate in ceremonial expression of the covenant in order to enjoy the core essence of the covenant. He could not bypass the name change and the circumcision and expect to enjoy the blessing of the covenant.

We cannot separate the two. We should not seek to separate thinking about the Lord's Supper from eating the elements (1 Corinthians 11:23-28). We cannot separate immersion from baptism (1 Peter 3:21). We cannot think the Lord's Supper into existence. We must participate in it. We cannot think baptism into existence. We must participate in it. A failure to participate in the ceremonial expression indicates ignorance or absence of integrity. The ceremonial expression of the covenant is inherently attached to the core essence of the covenant.

The term "baptism" never means sprinkle or pour, but to immerse (Acts 8:38-39; John 3:23; Matthew 27:57-60). It is not only important that baptism is practiced, but how it is practiced. It is a picture of our death, burial, and resurrection with Jesus (Romans 6:1-4). Baptism is an immersion. The fact of the definition and the fact of the illustration assure that (Acts 8:38-39). The wet side consists of a burial in water in order **to receive the benefits of the resurrection of Jesus** (1 Peter 3:21). Only when an immersion takes place for this purpose, is it valid (Acts 19:3-5).

God used the waters of the flood to save eight people during the days of Noah (1 Peter 3:20). What happens now? God uses the waters of baptism to save all who trust in the resurrection of Jesus Christ (1 Peter 3:21). The symbol preceded the real essence (Romans 5:14; Hebrews 9:24). The waters of the flood were a figure or type of baptism. Obviously, baptism consisted of that which one might think to be an external cleansing. Only if water was used, one might mistake baptism to be an external cleansing.

If you have experienced only the dry side, then you have only experienced half of a baptism. Half of a baptism is no baptism at all. You need to be immersed today. If you experienced only the wet side then there is no baptism at all. You need to be immersed today. The dry side must precede the wet side, and the wet side must follow the dry side for it to be a valid baptism. Baptism stands between you and salvation. God calls you to be baptized today.

**BECOME DEVOTED** – In order for a person to maximize the experience of salvation, he/she must become devoted to the instructions of the apostles. Now that you have been baptized into the body of Christ, you must learn to participate in kingdom practices so as to enjoy kingdom privileges. Always honor your kingdom citizenship.

Acts 2:41-42: On the day of Pentecost about 3,000 listeners received the word. To receive the word is to welcome the word (Luke 8:40). Those disciples who received and welcomed the word continually devoted themselves (remained faithfully in place, Acts 1:14, 2:46, 6:4, 8:13, 10:7).

They continually devoted themselves to the apostles' teachings [(doctrine, tutoring) Acts 2:42; Titus 1:9]. Teachings from the apostles originated with God (Acts 2:4; John 14:26, 7:16). Apostolic teachings were not stagnant, but were living principles that changed behavior and revolutionized the world.

They continually devoted themselves to fellowship (Acts 2:42). Through fellowship, they pledged their allegiance to each other. They expressed allegiance by participating in compatible activity because of their compatible interest (1 John 1:3, 6-7; 2 Corinthians 13:14; Philippians 2:1).

They continually devoted themselves to worship (Acts 2:42-43, 46a, 47). God wants our worship to become a matter of spiritual conviction. For us, worship should become more than just a matter of selfish convenience.

# WISDOM: WHAT YOU SHOULD HAVE LEARNED AS A TEENAGER BUT DIDN'T

JOHN MARSHALL

# Expand Your Knowledge with
## These Essential Reads by John Davis Marshall

*"Good and Angry"* - A Personal Guide to Anger Management

*"The Power of the Tongue"* – What You Say is What You Get

*"God, Listen"* – Prayers That God Always Answers [includes a 50-day addiction recovery guide]

*"Final Answer"* – You asked? God answered!

*"Success is a God Idea"*

*"Show Me the Money"* – 7 Exercises That Build Economic Strength.

*"God Knows"* – There is no Need to Worry.

*"My God"* – Who He is Will Change Your Life.

*"Faith, Family, & Finances" Vol. One* –. Essential Truths That Lead to Passionate Happiness.

*"Faith, Family, & Finances" Vol. Two* - The Mess We are in and How to Get Out of It!

*"A Queen In Search of A King"* – Go Ahead and Ask Him for a Date!

*"Church Matters"* – Passionate Pleadings That Prepare Us For The Future

*"Hallelujah"* – Worship Him According to His Preference

*"Called to be a Champion"* – Coaching Yourself Into the Champion Circle

*"Pre Marriage Preparations"* – From Me to We

*"Man HANDLE IT"*

*"Husband Love Your Wife"* – Even Though She Does Not Want You To

*"Wife be Subject to Your Husband"* – Even Though He Does Not Want You To

*"Reparations"* – Break the Poverty Cycle

*"Wisdom"* – Things I Should Have Learned When I Was A Teenager But Didn't

## www.JohnDavisMarshall.com

www.ingramcontent.com/pod-product-compliance
Lightning Source LLC
LaVergne TN
LVHW061555070526
838199LV00077B/7060